Anonymous

Standard atlas of Barry County, Michigan:

Including a plat book of the villages, cities and townships of the county

farmers directory, reference business directory and departments devoted

to general information

Anonymous

Standard atlas of Barry County, Michigan:
Including a plat book of the villages, cities and townships of the county farmers directory, reference business directory and departments devoted to general information

ISBN/EAN: 9783337713416

Printed in Europe, USA, Canada, Australia, Japan

Cover: Foto ©ninafisch / pixelio.de

More available books at **www.hansebooks.com**

STANDARD ATLAS

OF

BARRY COUNTY

MICHIGAN

INCLUDING
A PLAT BOOK
OF THE

VILLAGES, CITIES AND TOWNSHIPS OF THE COUNTY.
MAP OF THE STATE, UNITED STATES AND WORLD.
Farmers Directory, Reference Business Directory and Departments
devoted to General Information.
ANALYSIS OF THE SYSTEM OF U.S. LAND SURVEYS, DIGEST OF THE
SYSTEM OF CIVIL GOVERNMENT, ETC. ETC.

Compiled and Published
BY

GEO. A. OGLE & CO.

PUBLISHERS & ENGRAVERS.
134 VAN BUREN ST.
CHICAGO.

1895

Copyright 1895 by Geo. A. Ogle & Co.

TABLE OF CONTENTS.

GENERAL INDEX.

BARRY COUNTY INDEX.

OUTLINE MAP OF

BARRY COUNTY

MICHIGAN

Scale 4 miles of one Inch to one Mile

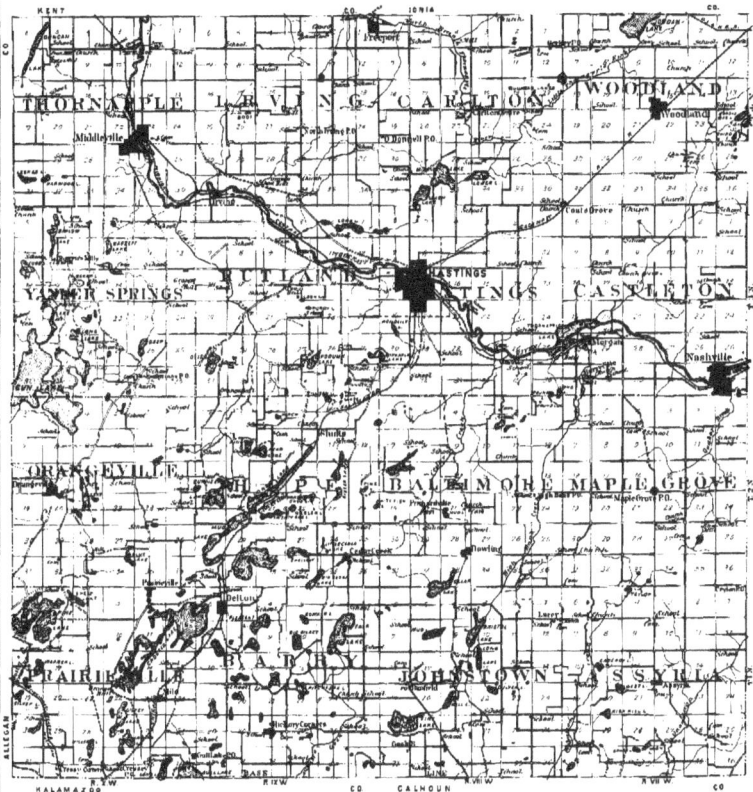

THORNAPLE   L R V I N G   CARLTON   WOODLAND

Middleville

YANKEE SPRINGS   BUTLER   HASTINGS   CASTLETON

Nashville

ORANGEVILLE   HOPE   BALTIMORE   MAPLE GROVE

PRAIRIEVILLE   BARRY   JOHNSTOWN   ASSYRIA

KENT   IONIA   CO.

KALAMAZOO   CALHOUN   CO

MAP OF
WOODLAND

Township 4 North   **Range 7 West**

Scale 2 Inches to one Mile   of the Meridian of Michigan

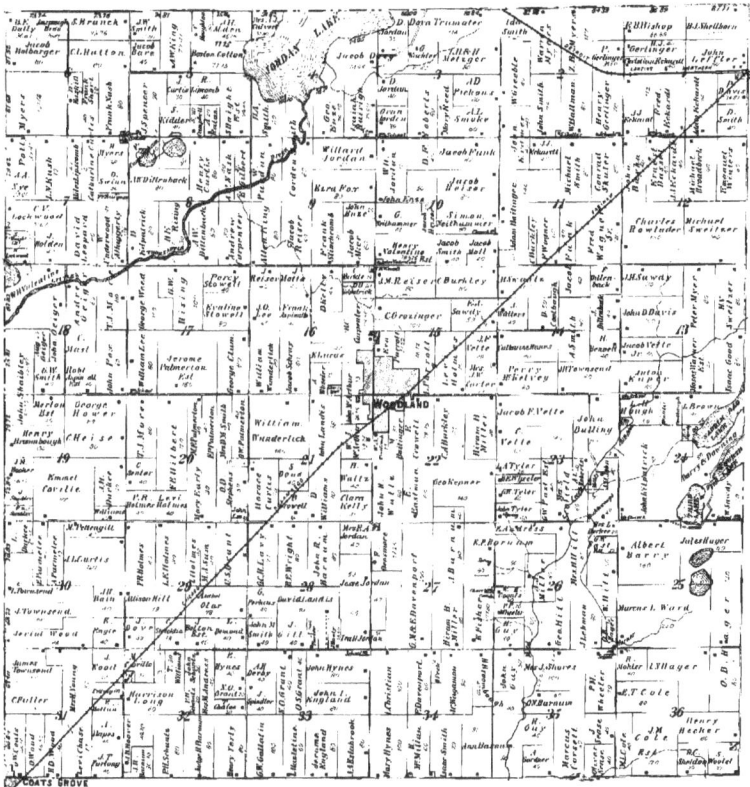

MAP OF
CARLTON

Township 4 North   Range 8 West

Scale 2 Inches to one Mile   of the Meridian of Michigan

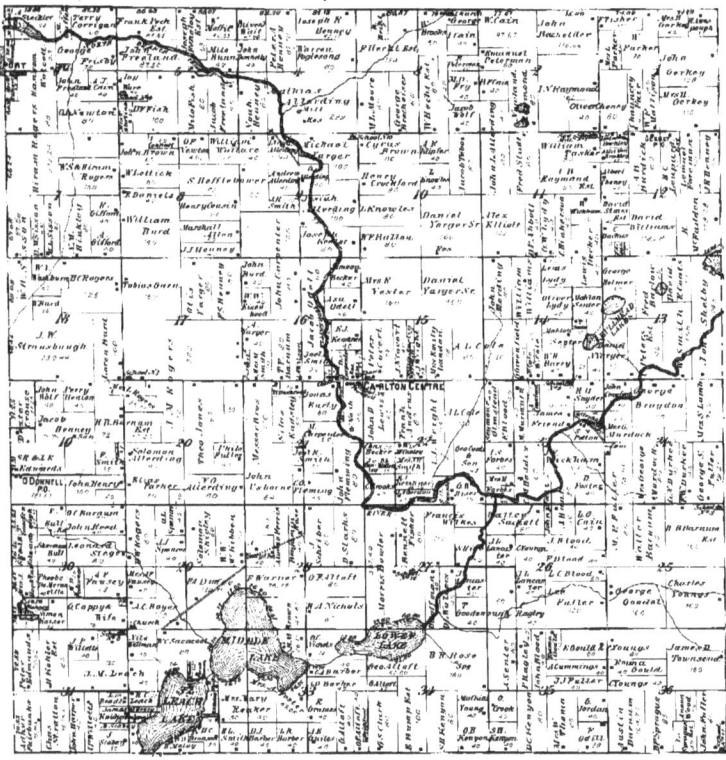

MAP OF
IRVING

Township 4 North   Range 9 West

Scale 2 Inches to one Mile.   of the Meridian of Michigan.

FREEDOM

IRVING MILL

MAP OF
THORNAPPLE

Township 4 North   Range 10 West

Scale 2 Inches to one Mile   of the Meridian of Michigan

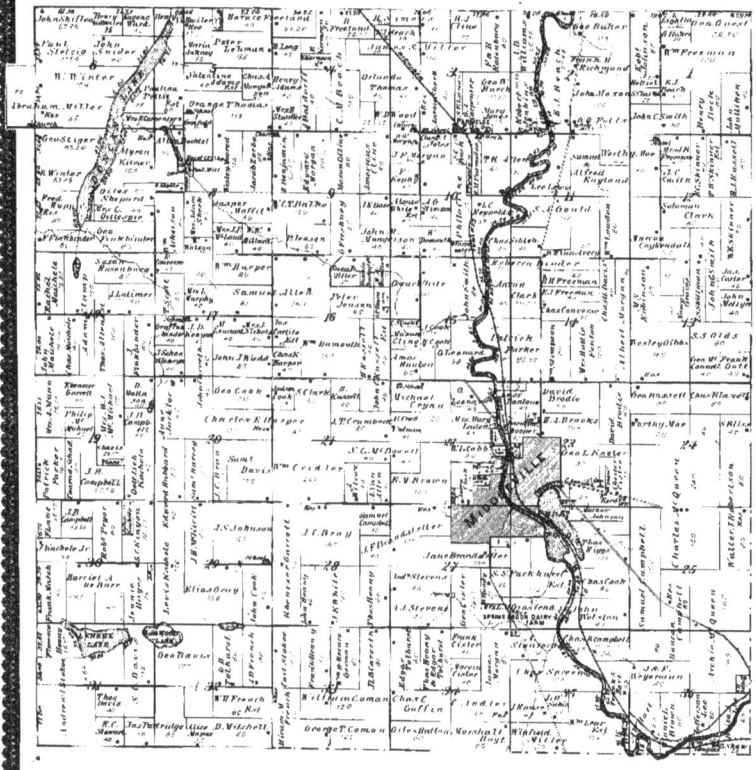

MAP OF
YANKEE SPRINGS

Township 3 North — Range 10 West

Scale 2 Inches to one Mile

of the Meridian of Michigan

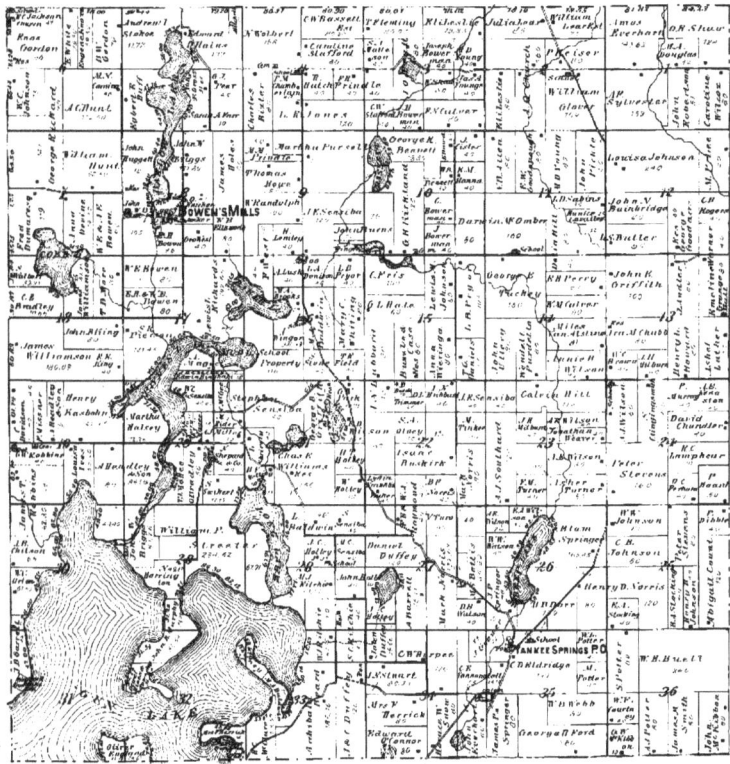

BOWEN'S MILLS

YANKEE SPRINGS P.O.

GUN LAKE

MAP OF
RUTLAND

Township 3 North   Range 9 West

Scale 2 Inches to one Mile   of the Meridian of Michigan

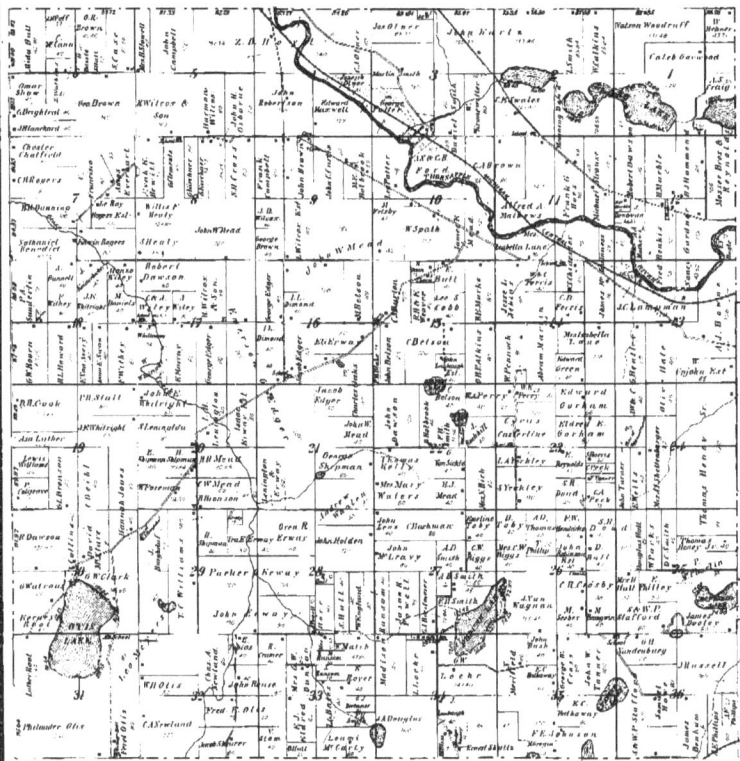

MAP OF
HASTINGS

Township 3 North   Range 8 West

Scale 2 Inches to one Mile

of the Meridian of Michigan

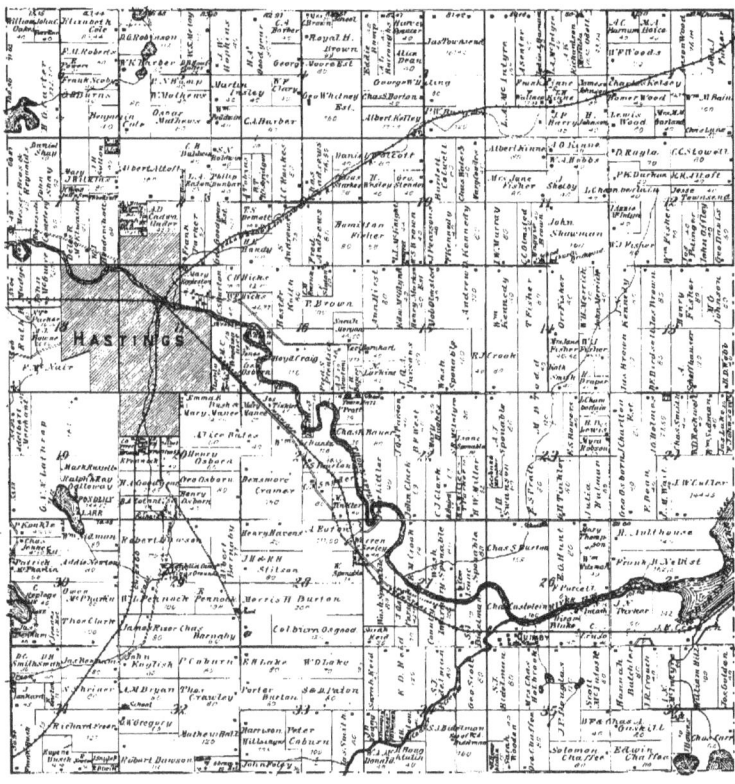

HASTINGS

MAP OF
CASTLETON

Township 3 North   **Range 7 West**

Scale 2 Inches to one Mile   of the Meridian of Michigan

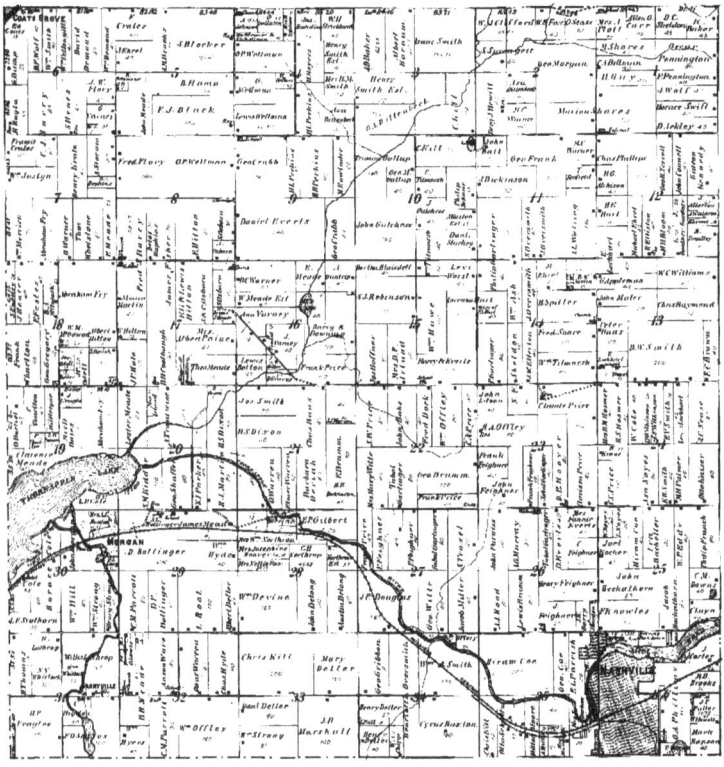

MAP OF
MAPLE GROVE

Township 2 North   Range 7 West

Scale 2 Inches to one Mile

of the Meridian of Michigan

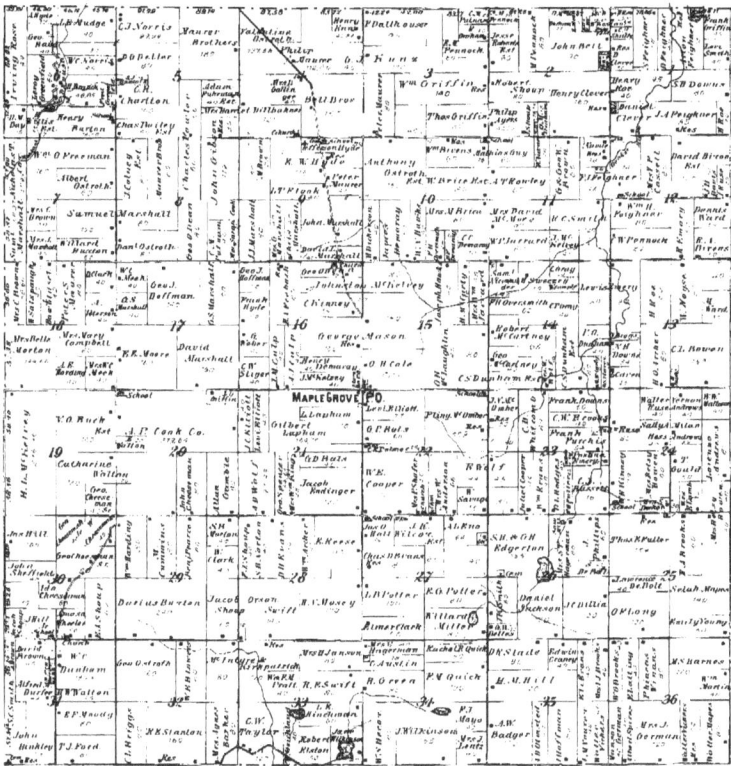

MAP OF
BALTIMORE

Township 2 North   Range 8 West

Scale 2 Inches to one Mile

of the Meridian of Michigan

DOWLING

RICHARDVILLE

HIGH BANK P.O.

MAP OF
HOPE

Township 2 North   Range 9 West

Scale 2 Inches to one Mile

of the Meridian of Michigan

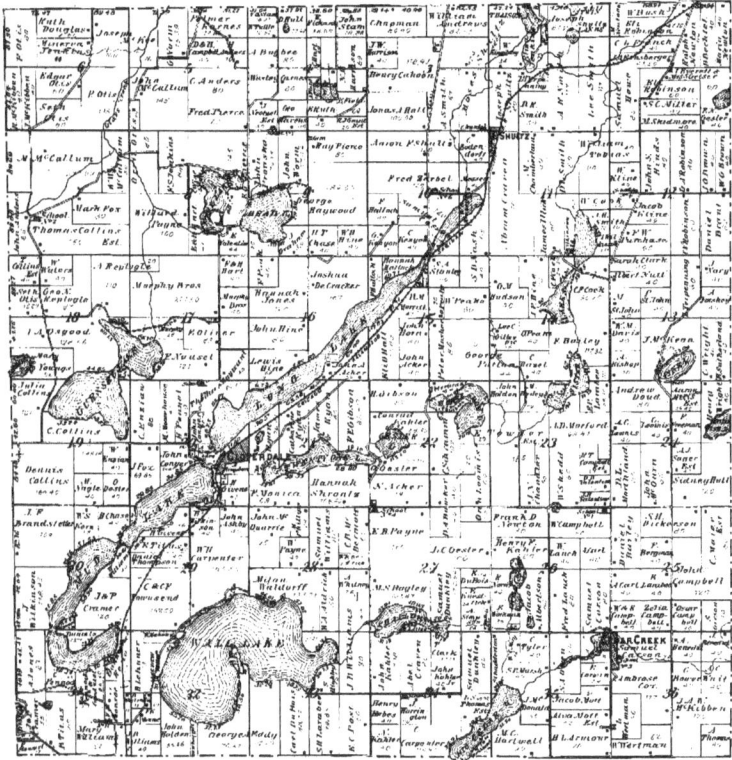

WALL LAKE

MAP OF
ORANGEVILLE

Township 2 North   Range 10 West

Scale 2 Inches to one Mile   of the Meridian of Michigan

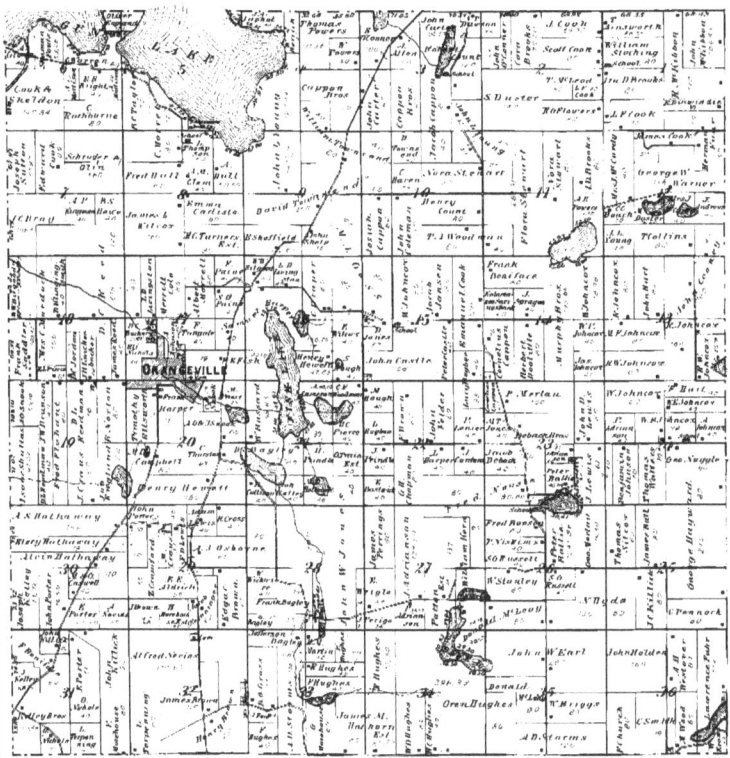

ORANGEVILLE

MAP OF
PRAIRIEVILLE

Township 1 North   Range 10 West

Scale 2 Inches to one Mile   of the Meridian of Michigan

L.B. Terpenning   W.Hughs & Son   W.Hughs   O.J.Hughs   Michael Baster   Mason   Music Church

Wyman J. Hull   McClinstey   PRAIRIEVILLE   W.L.Brown   Frank Wales

PINE LAKE   J.H.Freeman   Henry Starr   John   Mark Ward   Motten   HIGHLAND POINT

J.C.Morton   R.H. Marshall   J.H.Brandstetter   Michael Doster   M.M. Chase   Chase

Fred D. Wilson   Marr   Hannah James

C.F.Brainard   Udora Thompson   Willard D. Waters   A.Mills   J.Stanley Est.

Mrs.W.J Brouwel   P.Rogers   Augusta Baster   Robert Kay   W.H. Cutler

FOSTER   A.Royes   Kenyon & Kimmerer   Marvin Plower & Sons   J.C.Chase Est.

Jacob Tower   A.Francisco   R.H. Chase   H.W. Williams

Isaac Wilson   C.H.Honeywell   W.J. Williams

C.C.McLean   Thomas   F.Starr   Bennets   W.E. Towne

David Wilson   Edgar Mason   Robert Kay   Henry Fisher   James Ply

James Churchett   C.Cook   A.V. Davenport Est.   D.V.Penner   D.R.Penner   W.R.G. Downing

William Boolittle   J.W.Gilker   Henry Matthews   W.R.G. Downing   F.M.Mott

Charles Ruston   Arthur W. Shorter   H.H. Brownell   Nolan Barber   John Holden

John Barber   C.L.Barber

James Honeywell   David Reynolds Est.   Philip Barber   John Holden   GULL LAKE

MAP OF
BARRY

Township 1 North   Range 9 West

Scale 2 Inches to one Mile   of the Meridian of Michigan

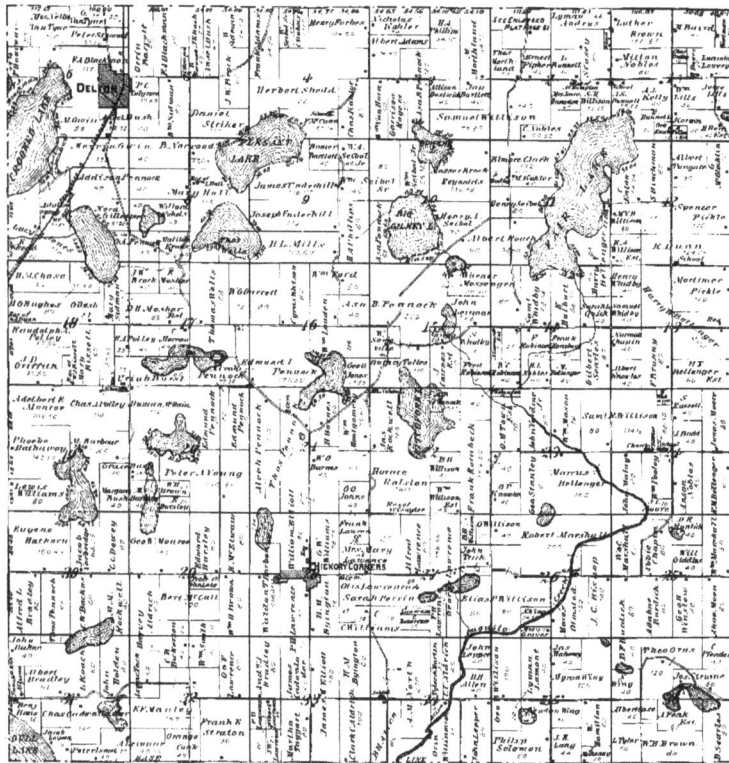

DELTON

HICKORY CORNERS

MAP OF
JOHNSTOWN

Township 1 North   Range 8 West

Scale 2 Inches to one Mile

of the Meridian of Michigan

MAP OF
ASSYRIA

Township 1 North   Range 7 West

Scale 2 Inches to one Mile   of the Meridian of Michigan

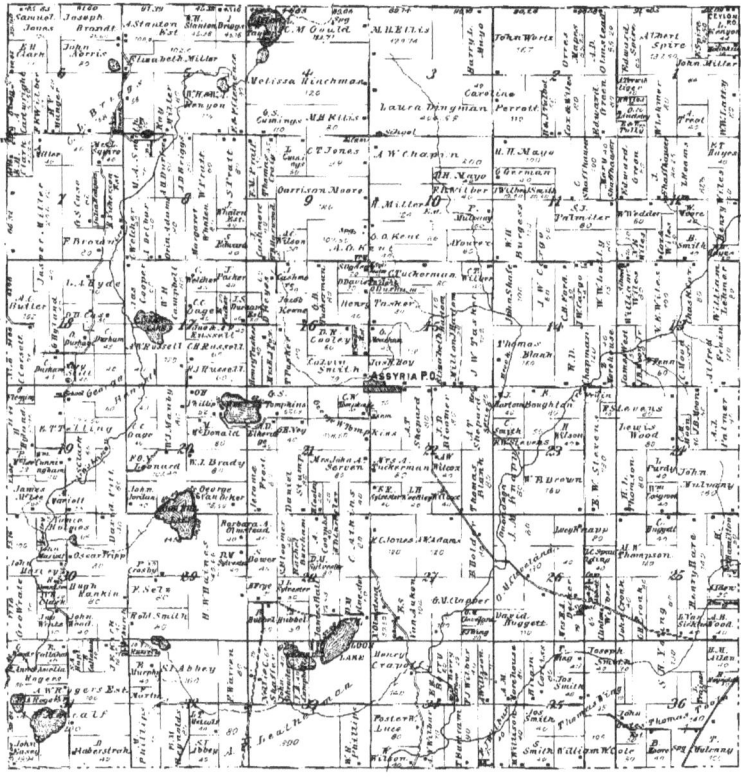

NORTH PART OF
HASTINGS
COUNTY SEAT OF BARRY CO. MICH.

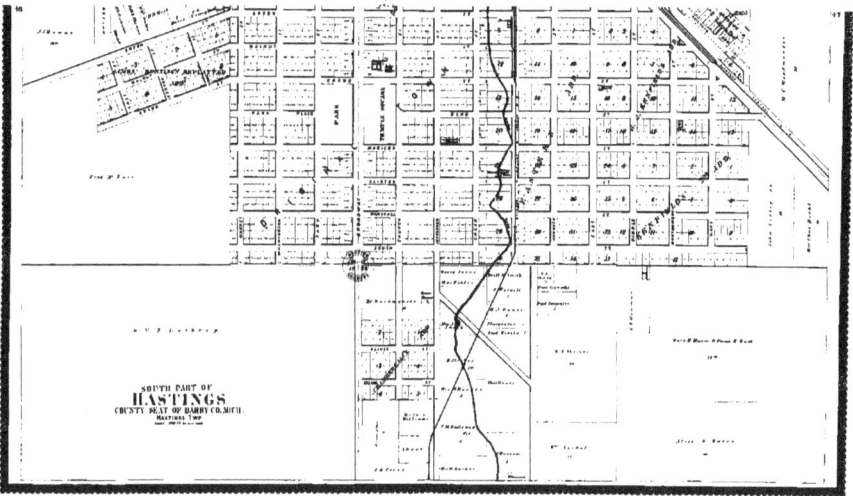

SOUTH PART OF
HASTINGS
COUNTY SEAT OF BARRY CO. MICH.
HASTINGS TWP

MIDDLEVILLE
THORNAPPLE TWP
Scale 400 ft. to 1 inch

53

Michael Cogan

Mary Logan
63

W. L. Cobb
.30

E. W. Brown
120

K. Harper Est.

Jacob Brandsteller

Soren Clark
30

Wallace Watson
9

David Matteson
8

Est. John C. Smith

J. Hollister
7

S. Abrams
4

Nelson Van Avery
500

Norris Ranch
10

David Hooper
30

A. D. Thomas

D. Brodie

A. P. Thomas

J. A. Gould

Chas. L. McLischy

H. J. Brooks
105

LAFAYETTE ST.

LINCOLN ST.

WASHINGTON ST.

DAYTON ST.

FREMONT

George L. Keeler ST.

M. S. Keeler

C. Annsson

SHERMAN ST.

JOHNSON ST.

MAIN ST.

FIRST ST.

SECOND ST.

THIRD ST.

FOURTH ST.

FIFTH ST.

DEARBORN ST.

STATE ST.

MARKET ST.

BROADWAY

ORIGINAL

MILL POND

June Brandsteller
105

S. S. Parkhurst Est.
1.92

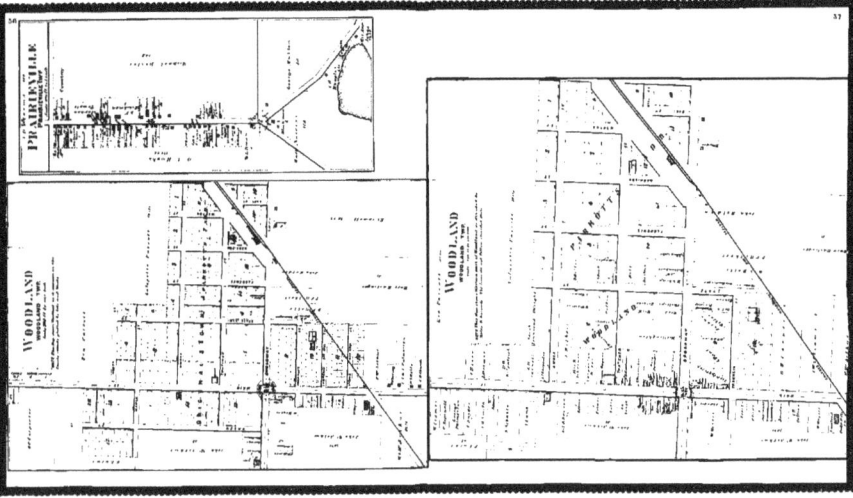

PRAIRIEVILLE

WOODLAND

WOODLAND

WOODLAND

DOWLING
BALTIMORE TWP.
Scale 300 ft. to 1 Inch.

J.E.Tobias 3

G.Nelson 4

W.H.Ormsbe 26

G.Wilson Est 2

C.Rice 3

J.H.Bacon 3

F.Webster 3

R.G.Rice

Dr F.G. Sheffield 3

N.E.Clemence 16

John E. Barrington

W.H.Ormsbe 2

Peter Jendro 32

John Herrington

A.J.Huffman

J.Reid

DELTON
BARRY TWP.
Scale 300 ft. to 1 Inch.
Ansel Bush

F.A.Blackman

FORD ST.

Livery

ORCHARD

MAPLE

LOW ST.

Eugene Horton

Mrs Geo Main

Geo Main

Mrs Evans

E.T.Colgrove

Ansel Bush

Orrin Morrell

HICKORY CORNERS
BARRY TWP.
Scale 300 Ft to 1 Inch

Geo W. Williams 28.75

Wm E.T.Lold

Jabez Rockwell

Helen M Ruck

M.W.

Church Property

Church Ground

P.H. Lawrence 77

Caldwallader

Schneider

J.W.Pine

L.H.Ware

P.H. Lawrence

W.H.Byington

IRVING
IRVING TWP.
Scale 300 ft. to 1 inch.

J.H.Jordan

A.D.Hughes & Co

Flour Mill

OAK ST.

OAK ST.

CHURCH

MILL ST.

ELM ST.

RACE

MAPLE ST.

CENTRAL

MICHIGAN

LONG LAKE

Eastand Brick Co

CENTER

A.Kingsbury

A.Kingsbury

MUD LAKE

H.Mosier

O.C.Conyer

Hannah Givens

CLOVERDALE
Hope Twp.
Scale 300 ft=1 inch.

John Ashby

C.Kingsbury

H.Wilkinson 40

John Ashby 40

Jus.Ryan

Fred Monroe

MORGAN
Platted as
SHERIDAN
CASTLETON TWP.
Scale 300 ft. to 1 inch.

E.Hale

Mrs.Alice L.Winslow

ST.

CENTRAL

RAILROAD

MAIN

HIGHLAND

JEFFERSON

MILL

EAST

ST.

D.Hollinger

John

Mrs.Alice L.Winslow

QUEEN

ST.

G.J.Long

HIGHLAND POINT
RESORT
Barton and Brandstetter Props.
PRAIRIEVILLE TWP.
Scale 300 feet to 1 inch.

CROOKED LAKE

F.A.Harkness

ASSYRIA
ASSYRIA TWP.
Scale 300 ft. to 1 inch.

C.Smith
A.W.
Wilcox

Barton

J.Abbey

School

W.A.Powers

James K.Hoy

W.Sage

School

Church

Oscar Crowfoot

J.Dron Wilson

J.Parks

G.W.Hopkins

Geo W.Tompkins

MILO
PRAIRIEVILLE TWP.
Scale 300 ft. to 1 inch.

Mrs.Addison Spaulding

GREEN

ST.

Mrs.M.Johnson

VINE

ST.

MAIN

ST.

Mrs.Jno Anson

C.N.Starr

ENLARGED PLAT
OF THE N.N.W.¼ SEC.3 BARRY TWP.
Scale 10 chains 1 inch.

Albert Hampton

Mortimer Hartwell

Northland

Mortimer
Hartwell

H.W.Elwain

ORANGEVILLE
ORANGEVILLE TWP.
Scale 300 ft = 1 inch.

C. Crawford

P. Tungate

A. Johnson

Eli Nichols

Robert Beattie

Beam Creek

UNION MAIN ST.

Reynold Mills Rd.

J. W. Bailey Rd.

F. & P.M. R.R.

CAMBRIDGE ST.

WATER

NICHOLS ST.

J. S. Pike

Cemetery

J. S. Pike

Eli Nichols 2.50

Mill Race

S. R. Cummings

Timothy Elsworth 70

J. M. Crane

Frank Harper 35

PRICHARDVILLE
BALTIMORE TWP.

Chas. Prichard 0.91

George Prichard 17.50

Wharton

P.O. Store

Bowens Hall

COAT'S GROVE
CASTLETON TWP.
Scale 300 ft to 1 inch.

Benson Coats

M. Ferris

Depot

F. R. Duskee

John J. Fuller

Rockford

Ed. Coats 18

PARMELEE
THORNAPPLE TWP.

Jacob Shank

Harmon

G. W. Bush

O. J. Carpenter 48

Mary Jones

Church

Store & P.O.

A. C. Buck 30

E. W. Parmelee 70

CEDAR CREEK
HOPE TWP.
Scale 300 ft to an inch.

W. H. B. Campbell

Campbell

W. V. Stanton

W. Bowman

C. F. Lamber

C. P. Larabee

C. P. Larabee

A. W. Pratt

C. P. Larabee

W. Fothergill

S. Carson 31

Eugene Corwin 20

C. Murphy

Sumner Creek

SHULTZ
HOPE TWP.

Jos. Shultz 20

J. Hasendorf

F. Barough

J. Cowman

GULL LAKE
PRAIRIEVILLE TWP.
Scale 300 ft to 1 inch.

G. P. Houns

F. Ginger 25

Mary Murphy 100

Ira McAllister 30.53

G. W. Thomas 125

Sarah Allison

Peter Creek

G. H. Taylor

Benjamin Potter Ginger Heirs

GULL LAKE

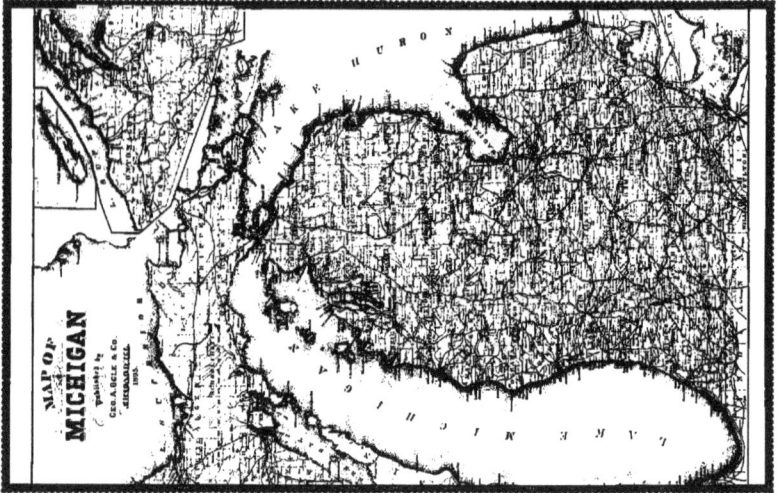

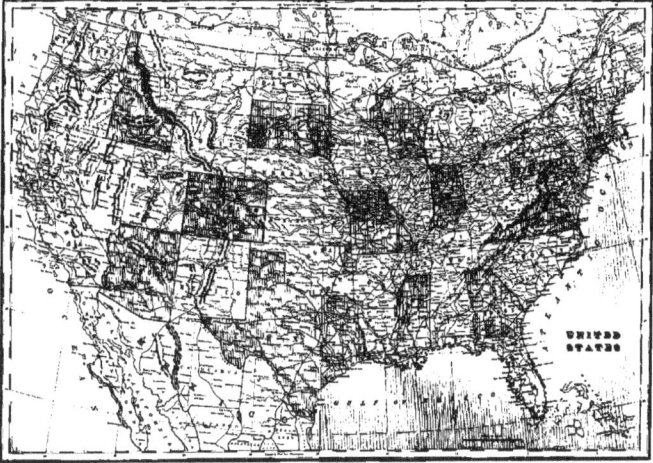

UNITED STATES

PRINCIPAL CITIES OF THE OLD WORLD.

CHART OF
THE WORLD

REFERENCE DIRECTORY

OF

BARRY ❖ COUNTY, ❖ MICHIGAN.

EXPLANATION. The date following a name indicates the length of time the party has been a resident of the county. The abbreviations are as follows: S. for Section; T. for Township; and P. O. for Post-office address. When no Section Number nor Township is given, it will be understood that the party resides within the limits of the village or city named, and, in such cases, the post-office address is the same as the place of residence, unless otherwise stated.

Lawrence, Albert, Farmer & Stock, S. 33, T. Barry, P. O. Hickory Corners, 1856.
Lawrence, P. H., Farmer, S. 28, T. Barry, P. O. Hickory Corners, 1852.
Leach, J. M., Farmer, S. 32, T. Carlton, P. O. Hastings, 1869.
Lee, Jefferson, Farmer, S. 34, T. Thornapple, P. O. Irving, 1855.
Lee, M. P., Farmer, S. 12, T. Yankee Springs, P. O. Irving, 1854.
Lee, Wm., Farmer, S. 17, T. Woodland, P. O. Woodland, 1855.
Lehner, Beulah, Farmer & Stock, S. 32, T. Hope, P. O. Delton, 1869.
Leinar, Jacob, Farmer, S. 22, T. Prairieville, P. O. Quincy, 1862.
Leinar, John, Farmer, S. 16, T. Barry, P. O. Hickory Corners, 1870.
Leinar, P., Farmer, S. 40, T. Hope, P. O. Shultz, 1866.
Leonard, Ezra, Farmer, S. 13, T. Irving, P. O. Freeport, 1852.
Leonard, P. O. R., Farmer, S. 20, T. Assyria, P. O. Assyria, 1853.
Leroy, P. J., Farmer, S. 25, T. Prairieville, P. O. Milo, 1860.
Lewis, Adam, Farmer, S. 29, T. Orangeville, P. O. Orangeville, 1856.
Lewis, David, Farmer, S. 1, T. Baltimore, P. O. Quimby, 1855.
Lewis, G. P., Farmer, S. 18, T. Baltimore, P. O. Hastings, 1865.
Lichty, John, Mngr. Poor Farm, S. 27, T. Hastings, P. O. Hastings, 1868.
Lindsay, Wm., Farmer, S. 5, T. Prairieville, P. O. Prairieville, 1874.
Little, Jesse, Farmer, S. 1, T. Barry, P. O. Cedar Creek, 1864.
Litts, Wm., Farmer, S. 1, T. Barry, P. O. Cedar Creek, 1864.
Litman, John, Farmer, S. 33, T. Castleton, P. O. Nashville, 1853.
Lockhart, E., Farmer, S. 12, T. Castleton, P. O. Nashville, 1878.
Loehr, G. W., Farmer, S. 34, T. Rutland, P. O. Hastings, 1868.
Loehr, L., Farmer, S. 34, T. Rutland, P. O. Hastings, 1870.
Long, R., Farmer, S. 4, T. Thornapple, P. O. Caledonia, 1864.
Long, S. R., Farmer, S. 31, T. Johnstown, P. O. Bedford, 1855.
Loudin, Wm., Farmer & Stock, S. 36, T. Barry, P. O. Hickory Corners, 1865.
Lowdon, W. O. (Lowdon & Barrell), Attorney at Law, Hastings, 1864.
Lowden, Wm., Farmer, S. 16, T. Thornapple, P. O. Middleville, 1855.
Lowry, G. W., Physician & Surgeon, Hastings, 1865.
Lunt, C. C., Merchant Tailor, Hastings, 1873.
Lutz, Philip, Shoemaker Manufacturing and Repairing, Hastings, 1867.
Lyons, S., Farmer, S. 29, T. Prairieville, P. O. Orangeville, 1863.
Lyon, W., Farmer, S. 18, T. Johnstown, P. O. Banfield, 1853.

Mack, C. M., Farmer, S. 29, T. Baltimore, P. O. Doetling, 1865.
Mahens, W., Farmer, S. 36, T. Hope, P. O. Delton, 1873.
Main, Geo., Farmer, S. 1, T. Johnstown, P. O. Banfield, 1860.
Maley, John S., Farmer & Stock, S. 24, T. Barry, P. O. Hickory Corners, 1855.
Mauet, O. H., Farmer, S. 11, T. Hastings, P. O. Hastings, 1866.
Manning, G. K., Farmer, S. 29, T. Baltimore, P. O. Doetling, 1862.
Manning, M. J., Farmer, S. 29, T. Baltimore, P. O. Doetling, 1855.
Manby, W. J., Farmer, S. 30, T. Assyria, P. O. Assyria, 1852.
Mapes, O., Farmer, S. 3, T. Assyria, P. O. Corlon, 1848.
Mapes, Walter, Farmer, S. 36, T. Maple Grove, P. O. Ceylon, 1862.
Marble, H. J., Justice of Peace & Farmer, S. 12, T. Rutland, P. O. Hastings, 1867.
Marble, W. I., Justice of Peace, Real Estate, Insurance, Loans, Oil Inspector, Nashville, 1869.
Marble, R. O., Farmer & Stock, S. 12, T. Rutland, P. O. Hastings, 1860.
Marinni, J., Farmer, S. 31, T. Johnstown, P. O. Bedford, 1851.
Marrinn, Jno., Farmer, S. 19, T. Assyria, P. O. Lacey, 1491.
Marsh, Frank, Farmer, S. 30, T. Thornapple, P. O. Middleville, 1867.
Marshall, Wm., Farmer & Stock, S. 20, T. Barry, P. O. Hickory Corners, 1862.
Marshall, Jacob, Farmer, S. 17, T. Maple Grove, P. O. Maple Grove, 1854.
Marshall, G. S., Farmer, S. 17, T. Maple Grove, P. O. Nashville, 1865.
Marshall, G. L., Farmer, S. 17, T. Maple Grove, P. O. Nashville, 1865.
Marshall, R. H., Farmer, S. 5, T. Prairieville, P. O. Prairieville, 1866.
Markmill, Robert, Retired Farmer, S. 23, T. Barry, P. O. Hickory Corners, 1843.
Martin, Bernard, Farmer, S. 7, T. Maple Grove, P. O. Nashville, 1872.
Martin, H. M., Farmer & Stock, S. 13, T. Orangeville, P. O. Prairieville, 1876.
Martin, Abram, Farmer, S. 14, T. Rutland, P. O. Hastings, 1851.
Mason, Geo., Farmer, S. 17, T. Maple Grove, P. O. Maple Grove, 1860.
Mason, Wm., Farmer, S. 33, T. Barry, P. O. Hickory Corners, 1859.
Mateh, William, Farmer & Stock, S. 34, T. Rutland, P. O. Hastings, 1863.
Mater, John, Farmer, S. 13, T. Castleton, P. O. Nashville, 1872.
Matthews, A. T., Farmer, S. 15, T. Rutland, P. O. Hastings, 1867.
Matthews, James, Farmer, S. 25, T. Baltimore, P. O. Lacey, 1866.
Matthews, N. A., All kinds of Musical Instruments, Pianos & Organs a specialty, Hastings, 1870.
Maurer, Peter, Farmer, S. 8, T. Maple Grove, P. O. Nashville, 1873.
Maurer, Philip, Farmer, S. 4, T. Maple Grove, P. O. Nashville, 1872.
Maurer, P. S., Farmer, S. 16, T. Maple Grove, P. O. Nashville, 1873.
Maxwell, E. L., Farmer, S. 4, T. Rutland, P. O. Hastings, 1862.
Mayo, H. M., Farmer, S. 1, T. Rutland, P. O. Hastings, 1848.
Mayo, H. L., Farmer, S. 5, T. Assyria, P. O. Ceylon, 1869.
McArthur, W. J., Farmer, S. 31, T. Woodland, P. O. Woodland, 1842.
McBain, Duncan, Farmer, S. 30, T. Barry, P. O. Hickory Corners.
McCall, Bart, Farmer, S. 29, T. Barry, P. O. Hickory Corners, 1860.
McCallum, John, Farmer, S. 8, T. Hope, P. O. Cloverdale, 1856.
McCallum, M., Farmer, S. 7, T. Hope, P. O. Cloverdale, 1842.
McCarragy, R., Farmer, S. 16, T. Maple Grove, P. O. Nashville, 1868.
McCoy, Archie, Dealer in Furniture, Carpets, Etc., Hastings, 1866.
McDerby, Frank, Grocer, Toys, Supervisor, Nashville, 1876.
McDermott, C. B., Farmer, S. 3, T. Hope, P. O. Cloverdale, 1866.
McDonald, A., Farmer & Stock, S. 1, T. Baltimore, P. O. Quimby, 1863.
McDonald, G. W., Farmer, S. 15, T. Hope, P. O. Cedar Creek, 1870.
McDonald, J., Farmer, S. 36, T. Hope, P. O. Cedar Creek, 1856.
McDowell, J., Farmer, S. 21, T. Thornapple, P. O. Middleville, 1879.
McErwin, D. R., Farmer, S. 5, T. Hastings, P. O. Hastings, 1854.
McFadden, G. H., Farmer, S. 13, T. Carlton, P. O. Shelbyville, 1865.
McFarland, Wm., Farmer, S. 12, T. Barry, P. O. Banfield, 1875.
McGuinness, Jason, Farmer, S. 14, T. Hastings, P. O. Hastings, 1866.
McGuire, John, Farmer, S. 36, T. Hope, P. O. Cedar Creek, 1864.
McIntosh, Scott, Farmer, S. 15, T. Hastings, P. O. Quimby, 1873.
McIntyre, J., Farmer, S. 3, T. Maple Grove, P. O. Maple Grove, 1867.
McIntyre, L. A., Farmer, S. 4, T. Hastings, P. O. Hastings, 1879.
McKelvey, J., Postmaster, S. 15, T. Maple Grove, P. O. Maple Grove, 1855.
McKenzie, J., Farmer, S. 27, T. Johnstown, P. O. Banfield, 1866.
McKevitt, James H., Sheriff Barry County, Hastings, 1865.
McKloin, W. H., Farmer, S. 29, T. Carlton, P. O. Hastings, 1867.
McKnight, L. L., Farmer, S. 16, T. Hastings, P. O. Hastings, 1872.
McLauhy, Chas. L., Retired, Middleville, 1871.
McNett, G. H., Farmer, S. 10, T. Rutland, P. O. Hastings, 1858.
McParker, Philip, Farmer & Stock, S. 22, T. Maple Grove, P. O. Maple Grove, 1858.
McPeak, Richard, Farmer, S. 12, T. Baltimore, P. O. Doetling, 1861.
McPharLin, P., Farmer, S. 20, T. Hastings, P. O. Hastings, 1859.
McQuartie, John, Farmer, S. 36, T. Hope, P. O. Delton, 1866.
McQueEn, Archie, Farmer, S. 33, T. Thornapple, P. O. Middleville, 1843.
McQueen, Chas., Farmer, S. 33, T. Thornapple, P. O. Middleville, 1862.
McQueen, John, Farmer, S. 33, T. Thornapple, P. O. Middleville, 1852.
Mead, H. H., Farmer, S. 20, T. Rutland, P. O. Nashville, 1855.
Mead, J. J., Farmer, S. 22, T. Rutland, P. O. Hastings, 1868.
Mead, J. W., Farmer, S. 14, T. Rutland, P. O. Hastings, 1866.
Mead, W., Farmer, S. 14, T. Castleton, P. O. Morgan, 1865.
Meade, S., Farmer, S. 7, T. Castleton, P. O. Hastings, 1867.
Meade, Thos., Farmer, S. 17, T. Castleton, P. O. Nashville, 1852.
Merck, W. H., Farmer, S. 1, T. Hastings, P. O. Hastings, 1866.
Merrick, W. H., Farmer, S. 14, T. Hastings, P. O. Hastings, 1865.

Merrifield, N., Farmer, S. 33, T. Rutland, P. O. Hastings, 1859.
Merrill, F. J., Farmer, Road Commissioner, S. 35, T. Johnstown, P. O. Banfield, 1860.
Merrill, G. A., Farmer, S. 34, T. Rutland, P. O. Shultz, 1893.
Merrill, H. T., Farmer, S. 16, T. Johnstown, P. O. Banfield, 1856.
Messer, Chester, Vice-President Hastings City Bank, Hastings, 1842.
Meyers, Wesley, Druggist, Toys, Clerk & Notary, Woodland, 1848.
Miller, Abraham, Farmer & Stock, S. 8, T. Thornapple, P. O. Caledonia, 1871.
Miller, George, Farmer & Stock, S. 11, T. Johnstown, P. O. Lacey, 1856.
Miller, Martin, Farmer & Stock, S. 22, T. Johnstown, P. O. Bedford, 1860.
Miller, A. J., Farmer, S. 7, T. Assyria, P. O. Lacey, 1867.
Miller, H. W., Farmer, S. 32, T. Hastings, P. O. Hastings, 1872.
Miller, Jacob, Farmer, S. 27, T. Castleton, P. O. Nashville, 1863.
Miller, J. R., Farmer, S. 1, T. Thornapple, P. O. Parmelee, 1875.
Miller, Jasper, Farmer, S. 7, T. Assyria, P. O. Lacey, 1852.
Miller, J. A., Farmer, S. 30, T. Woodland, P. O. Woodland, 1856.
Miller, W. G., Farmer, S. 27, T. Maple Grove, P. O. Nashville, 1866.
Miller, Winfield, Farmer, S. 32, T. Thornapple, P. O. Middleville, 1876.
Miner, G. S., Farmer, S. 10, T. Yankee Springs, P. O. Bowens Mills, 1872.
Moffit, Wm. Jasper, Minister, S. 6, T. Thornapple, P. O. Middleville, 1862.
Monroe, A. E., Farmer, S. 29, T. Barry, P. O. Hickory Corners, 1854.
Moody, E. T., Farmer, S. 15, T. Maple Grove, P. O. Lacey, 1855.
Moon, Abial, Farmer, S. 23, T. Barry, P. O. Hickory Corners, 1854.
Moon, C. T., Farmer, S. 24, T. Assyria, P. O. Bellevue, 1852.
Moon, J. T., Farmer, S. 26, T. Baltimore, P. O. High Bank, 1870.
Moon, C. W., Farmer, S. 6, T. Johnstown, P. O. Banfield, 1855.
Moore, E. M., Farmer, S. 19, T. Maple Grove, P. O. Maple Grove, 1861.
Moore, James, Farmer, S. 16, T. Irving, P. O. Freeport, 1853.
Moore, J. I., Farmer, S. 24, T. Barry, P. O. Banfield, 1867.
Moreau, C., Farmer, S. 27, T. Hope, P. O. Cedar Creek, 1846.
Morgan, J. F., Farmer, S. 16, T. Thornapple, P. O. Parmelee, 1863.
Morgan, John, Farmer, S. 36, T. Castleton, P. O. Dowling, 1874.
Morgan, M. S., Farmer, S. 35, T. Castleton, P. O. Dowling, 1874.
Morehouse, Moward, Railway Agent & General Merchant, Cloverdale, 1866.
Moerher, Peter, Farmer, S. 15, T. Hope, P. O. Cloverdale, 1856.
Mosey, Jacob, Farmer, S. 36, T. Hope, P. O. Cedar Creek, 1862.
Moulton, G. W., Farmer, S. 11, T. Irving, P. O. Freeport, 1848.
Moulton, R., Farmer, S. 17, T. Irving, P. O. Freeport, 1853.
Moulton, J. W., Farmer, S. 14, T. Irving, P. O. Freeport, 1848.
Mowry, C. M., Farmer, S. 6, T. Baltimore, P. O. Cedar Creek, 1876.
Mowry, Edward, Farmer, S. 6, T. Baltimore, P. O. Cedar Creek, 1870.
Mowell, John, Farmer, S. 17, T. Thornapple, P. O. Parmelee, 1867.
Mudge, D. L., Propr. Feed Meat, Hastings, 1865.
Muggridge, Wm., Farmer, S. 30, T. Irving, P. O. Middleville, 1864.
Muir, Grant, Farmer, S. 31, T. Rutland, P. O. Hastings, 1862.
Mullaly, John, Farmer, S. 24, T. Assyria, P. O. Bellevue, 1864.
Mulvany, T., Farmer, S. 36, T. Assyria, P. O. Bellevue, 1864.
Mulvany, J. F., Farmer & Stock, S. 36, T. Assyria, P. O. Bellevue, 1859.
Mumford, J. W., Farmer, S. 30, T. Thornapple, P. O. Middleville, 1874.
Mundock, A., Farmer, S. 35, T. Orangeville, P. O. Orangeville, 1860.
Murphy, Edward, Farmer, S. 17, T. Hope, P. O. Cloverdale, 1856.
Murphy, James, Farmer, S. 17, T. Hope, P. O. Cloverdale, 1850.
Murphy, A. O., Farmer, S. 17, T. Carleton, P. O. Nashville, 1865.
Murray, J., Farmer, S. 7, T. Irving, P. O. Freeport, 1843.
Murray, E., Farmer, S. 11, T. Rutland, P. O. Hastings, 1860.
Murray, R. W., Farmer, S. 4, T. Baltimore, P. O. Hastings, 1860.
Myers, M., Farmer, S. 4, T. Baltimore, P. O. Cedar Creek, 1876.
Myers, Leo, Farmer, S. 32, T. Rutland, P. O. Hastings, 1868.

Naggley, John G., County Clerk & Clerk of Court, Hastings, 1858.
Narbin, T., Farmer, S. 31, T. Thornapple, P. O. Parmelee, 1863.
National Bank of Battle Creek, General Banking, Battle Creek.
Neham, Geo. M. (Temple & Neham), Merchant, Genl. Mdse., Prairieville, 1850.
Nelson, D. E., Farmer, S. 17, T. Rutland, P. O. Shultz, 1869.
Newland, C. A., Farmer, S. 33, T. Rutland, P. O. Hastings, 1860.
Newton, D. G., Farmer, S. 35, T. Hastings, P. O. Hastings, 1857.
Newton, H. A., Milk-man, Niagara Print, Etc., Hastings, 1867.
Newton, J. G., Farmer, S. 17, T. Irving, P. O. Freeport, 1861.
Nichols, Eli, Merchant, General Merchandise, Orangeville, 1817.
Nichols, C. P., Farmer, S. 31, T. Orangeville, P. O. One Marsh, 1845.
Nichols, Willard, Farmer, S. 9, T. Barry, P. O. Delton, 1867.
Nicholson, L., Farmer & Stock, S. 1, T. Barry, P. O. Banfield, 1856.
Noble, Milton, Farmer & Stock, S. 30, T. Barry, P. O. Hickory Corners, 1856.
Noble, H. L., Farmer, S. 18, T. Barry, P. O. Hickory Corners, 1856.
Norris, O. J., Farmer & Stock, S. 7, T. Hastings, P. O. Morgan, 1861.
Norris, II. D., Farmer, S. 20, T. Yankee Springs, P. O. Yankee Springs, 1879.
North, J. H., Farmer, S. 5, T. Assyria, P. O. Lacey, 1854.
Norris, Mark, Farmer, S. 22, T. Prairieville, P. O. Prairieville, 1844.
Norris, H., Farmer, S. 22, T. Prairieville, P. O. Prairieville, 1844.
Norton, G. A., Farmer, S. 12, T. Maple Grove, P. O. Maple Grove, 1863.
Norton, S., Farmer, S. 31, T. Irving, P. O. North Irving, 1866.
Norton, Robert, Farmer, S. 31, T. Orangeville, P. O. Orangeville, 1851.
Norton, A. E., Farmer, S. 38, T. Irving, P. O. Delton, 1856.
Noyce, Asa, Farmer, S. 24, T. Thornapple, P. O. Nashville, 1865.
Nusel, Gotthart, Farmer & Stock, S. 20, T. Johnstown, P. O. Hope, P. O. Middleville, 1856.
Nye, A. B., Farmer, S. 9, T. Prairieville, P. O. Milo, 1864.
Nye, W. B., Farmer, S. 9, T. Prairieville, P. O. Orangeville, 1867.

Oaks, Chas., Farmer & Stock, S. 30, T. Rutland, P. O. Hastings, 1854.
Oakley, J., Farmer & Stock, S. 30, T. Rutland, P. O. Hastings, 1852.
Odell, Jacob, Farmer, S. 6, T. Carlton, P. O. Carlton Center, 1842.
Odell, W. A., Farmer, S. 8, T. Carlton, P. O. Nashville, 1860.
Ohlman, J., Farmer, S. 27, T. Carlton, P. O. Nashville, 1864.
Ohmer, G. T., Farmer, S. 17, T. Castleton, P. O. Nashville, 1891.
Orangeville School, Incl. Nunken, S. 15, T. Orangeville, P. O. Orangeville.
Orion, W. F., Farmer, S. 4, T. Castleton, P. O. Hastings, 1859.
Osborn, Ad., Farmer, S. 8, T. Carlton, P. O. Carlton Center, 1865.
Osborn, J. H., Farmer, S. 8, T. Carlton, P. O. Dowling, 1862.
Osborn, John, Farmer, S. 7, T. Baltimore, P. O. Dowling, 1861.
Osgood, C. H., Farmer, S. 4, T. Baltimore, P. O. Cedar Creek, 1867.
Osgood, M., Farmer, S. 16, T. Baltimore, P. O. Cedar Creek, 1860.
Osgood, J. A., Farmer, S. 34, T. Prairieville, P. O. Orangeville, 1851.
Osgood, L., Farmer, S. 36, T. Hope, P. O. Cloverdale, 1866.
Osgood, R., Farmer, S. 6, T. Irving, P. O. Cloverdale, 1860.
Osterout, Valentine, Farmer, S. 4, T. Maple Grove, P. O. Nashville, 1865.
Otis, Fred, Farmer & Stock, S. 12, T. Rutland, P. O. Nashville, 1858.
Otis, Geo., Farmer, S. 8, T. Rutland, P. O. Hastings, 1867.
Otis, O. J., Farmer, S. 8, T. Hope, P. O. Shultz, 1863.
Otis, Philander, Farmer, S. 11, T. Rutland, P. O. Hastings, 1855.

Packard, J. E., Farmer & Stock, S. 30, T. Hastings, P. O. Hastings, 1890.
Packard, J. R., Farmer, S. 28, T. Hastings, P. O. Hastings, 1893.

Padelford, G. H., Farmer, S. 13, T. Baltimore, P. O. High Bank, 1857.
Page, Henry, Farmer, S. 36, T. Yankee Springs, P. O. Yankee Springs, 1873.
Palmer, C. R., Farmer & Stock, S. 22, T. Maple Grove, P. O. Maple Grove, 1865.
Palmer, H. F., Farmer, S. 17, T. Irving, P. O. Middleville, 1864.
Palmerton, C. B., Attorney at Law & Notary Public, Woodland, 1851.
Palmerton, J. P., Farmer, S. 30, T. Woodland, P. O. Woodland, 1855.
Parker, R. T., Propr. Hastings House, Hotel & Livery, Hastings, 1847.
Parmer, Mercer, Farmer, S. 27, T. Hastings, 1867.
Parrott, C. M., Farmer & Stock, S. 32, T. Castleton, P. O. Morgan, 1854.
Partridge, James, Farmer, S. 34, T. Thornapple, P. O. Middleville, 1864.
Paschen, J. C., Farmer, S. 4, T. Assyria, P. O. Lacey, 1860.
Patee, D., Farmer, S. 11, T. Hastings, P. O. Hastings, 1862.
Paton, S., Farmer, S. 35, T. Hastings, P. O. Hastings, 1867.
Patten, Wm. H., Attorney at Law, Hastings.
Payer, E. O., Farmer & Stock, S. 27, T. Hope, P. O. Cloverdale, 1875.
Payne, C. E., Farmer, S. 23, T. Hope, P. O. Cloverdale, 1860.
Payne, C. B., Farmer, S. 27, T. Hope, P. O. Cloverdale, 1870.
Payne, Daniel, Farmer, S. 27, T. Hope, P. O. Cloverdale, 1870.
Payne, J. A., Farmer, S. 16, T. Hastings, P. O. Hastings, 1862.
Payne, W. M., Farmer, S. 8, T. Hope, P. O. Cloverdale, 1873.
Peake, W. J., Farmer, S. 15, T. Hope, P. O. Shultz, 1862.
Peaee, J., Farmer, S. 29, T. Maple Grove, P. O. Maple Grove, 1852.
Peck, C. A., Farmer, S. 23, T. Rutland, P. O. Hastings, 1853.
Peckham, M. P., Physician & Surgeon, Freeport, 1862.
Peesols, Henry, S. 23, T. Prairieville, P. O. Milo, 1866.
Pennington, Capt. Farmer, S. 1, T. Castleton, P. O. Nashville, 1876.
Pennock, A. J., Farmer, S. 7, T. Barry, P. O. Delton, 1859.
Pennock C., Farmer, S. 36, T. Hope, P. O. Delton, 1855.
Pennock, G. S., Farmer, S. 12, T. Maple Grove, P. O. Nashville, 1867.
Pennock, S., Farmer, S. 26, T. Hastings, P. O. Hastings, 1848.
Pennock, H., Farmer, S. 7, T. Maple Grove, P. O. Nashville, 1870.
Pennock, E. L., Farmer, S. 6, T. Barry, P. O. Hickory Corners, 1854.
Pennock, M., Farmer, S. 2, T. Maple Grove, P. O. Nashville, 1844.
Pennock W. L., Farmer, S. 26, T. Hastings, P. O. Hastings, 1861.
Perham, J. J., Farmer & Stock, S. 31, T. Maple Grove, P. O. Nashville, 1864.
Perkins, J. J., Farmer, S. 1, T. Prairieville, P. O. Prairieville, 1856.
Perkins, R. W., Farmer, S. 23, T. Barry, P. O. Delton, 1860.
Perry, W. E., Farmer, S. 33, T. Rutland, P. O. Hastings, 1865.
Perry, W. F., Farmer, S. 33, T. Rutland, P. O. Hastings, 1876.
Peringill, Wm., Farmer, S. 6, T. Castleton, P. O. Grass Grove, 1867.
Phelps, E. L., Livery, Feed & Sale Stables, Middleville.
Phillips, A. R., Farmer, S. 36, T. Rutland, P. O. Hastings, 1871.
Phillips, A. F., Farmer, S. 36, T. Rutland, P. O. Hastings, 1871.
Phillips, C. D., Farmer, S. 17, T. Maple Grove, P. O. Nashville, 1849.
Phillips, H. A., Farmer, S. 5, T. Barry, P. O. Hickory Corners, 1860.
Phillips, J. H., Farmer, S. 25, T. Baltimore, P. O. Dowling, 1864.
Phillips, Chas. Farmer, Nashville, 1862.
Phillips, J. C., Propr. Johnstown, P. O. Banfield, 1868.
Pilley, Robert, Farmer, S. 11, T. Barry, P. O. Banfield, 1850.
Pierce, John, Farmer, S. 17, T. Johnstown, P. O. Banfield, 1854.
Pinkerton, J. M., Farmer, S. 16, T. Castleton, P. O. Casball, 1863.
Pike, C. T., Miller & Grain, S. 7, T. Thornapple, P. O. Caledonia, 1864.
Pike, C. F., Farmer, S. 26, T. Assyria, P. O. Bellevue, 1864.
Pingree, Sewell, Farmer & Stock, S. 30, T. Assyria, P. O. Assyria, 1862.
Pullen C. A., Farmer, S. 34, T. Barry, P. O. Hickory Corners, 1846.
Pulleo, E. A., Farmer, S. 34, T. Barry, P. O. Hickory Corners, 1846.
Porter, C. A., Farmer & Stock, S. 30, T. Johnstown, P. O. Banfield, 1852.
Post, F. C., Farmer, S. 33, T. Hope, P. O. Delton, 1860.
Potter, Geo. H. Farmer & Cheese Manufacturer, S. 3, T. Rutland, P. O. Hastings, 1876.
Potter, E. G., Farmer, S. 27, T. Maple Grove, P. O. Nashville, 1861.
Potter, L. B., Farmer, S. 27, T. Maple Grove, P. O. Maple Grove, 1869.
Powers, Wm. H., Attorney & Assistant Prosecutor Hastings City Bank, Hastings, 1858.
Powers, W. M., Farmer, S. 33, T. Rutland, P. O. Lacey, 1861.
Powers, W. S., Lawyer, Nashville, 1863.
Pratt, H. G., Farmer, S. 17, T. Yankee Springs, P. O. Middleville, 1869.
Pringle, Henry, Farmer, S. 21, T. Baltimore, P. O. Cedar Creek, 1860.
Prindle, Fred, S. 8, T. Maple Grove, P. O. Nashville, 1878.
Prior, Frank, Farmer, Fruits, Fine Stock, S. 25, T. Baltimore, P. O. Nashville, 1868.
Price, Chandler, Farmer, S. 34, T. Castleton, P. O. Nashville, 1867.
Price, Clayton, Farmer, S. 30, T. Irving, P. O. Freeport, 1865.
Price, S. A. Farmer, S. 4, T. Irving, P. O. North Irving, 1848.
Prindle, Charles, Farmer & Stock, S. 16, T. Irving, P. O. North Irving, 1864.
Pritchard, Albert, Farmer & Stock, S. 24, T. Baltimore, P. O. Dowling, 1866.
Pruchen, E. T., Farmer, S. 30, T. Irving, P. O. Middleville, 1858.
Pryor, Robert, Farmer, S. 30, T. Maple Grove, P. O. Nashville, 1863.

Ragle, H., Farmer & Stock, S. 19, T. Castleton, P. O. Castleton, 1860.
Raldy, J., Farmer, S. 12, T. Maple Grove, P. O. Nashville, 1868.
Ransom, S. S., Farmer, S. 12, T. Maple Grove, P. O. Nashville, 1869.
Ransom, J., Farmer, S. 31, T. Rutland, P. O. Hastings, 1853.
Raynor, C. S., Farmer, S. 30, T. Yankee Springs, P. O. Yankee Springs, 1862.
Raymond, F. R., Farmer, S. 22, T. Hastings, P. O. Hastings, 1865.
Reas, Wm., Farmer, S. 16, T. Hastings, P. O. Hastings, 1867.
Reed, J. L., Carriage Maker & Repairer, Hastings, 1866.
Reed, James, Farmer, S. 5, T. Irving, P. O. Middleville, 1851.
Reed, F. W., Farmer, S. 24, T. Baltimore, P. O. Dowling, 1865.
Reed, A. H., Farmer, S. 5, T. Irving, P. O. North Irving, 1866.
Rood, E. D., Farmer, S. 17, T. Irving, P. O. North Irving, 1863.
Reed, Alonzo, Farmer, S. 17, T. Hope, P. O. Shultz, 1855.
Reid, James, Farmer, S. 7, T. Hastings, P. O. Hastings, 1869.
Reeliy, W., Farmer, S. 36, T. Johnstown, P. O. Banfield, 1876.
Remington, O. Farmer, Thornapple.
Rennolds, M. T., Farmer & Stock, S. 15, T. Barry, P. O. Hickory Corners.
Reynolds, James H. S., Farmer, S. 15, T. Barry, P. O. Hickory Corners.
Rice, C. R., Farmer, S. 6, T. Baltimore, P. O. Cedar Creek, 1867.
Rice, C. F., Farmer, S. 6, T. Baltimore, P. O. Cedar Creek, 1867.
Rice, Wm., Farmer, S. 34, T. Castleton, P. O. Nashville, 1852.
Rich, M., Farmer & Stock, S. 17, T. Johnstown, P. O. Bedford, 1856.
Richmond, L. J., Farmer, S. 25, T. Baltimore, P. O. Dowling, 1860.
Riley, Geo., Farmer, S. 36, T. Johnstown, P. O. Banfield, 1856.
Riley, M., Farmer, S. 28, T. Yankee Springs, P. O. Yankee Springs, 1862.

Williams, B. L., Farmer, S. 23, T. Hope, P. O. Delton, 1652.
Williams, T. C., Farmer, S. 29, T. Rutland, P. O. Hastings, 1650.
Williams, Wm., Farmer, S. 14, T. Carlton, P. O. Carlton Centre, 1860.
Williams, A., Farmer, S. 25, T. Assyria, P. O. Battle Creek, 1858.
Williams, S. H., Farmer, S. 22, T. Barry, P. O. Hickory Corners, 1852.
Williams, Geo. E., Farmer & Stock, S. 26, T. Barry, P. O. Hickory Corners, 1851.
Willison, Samuel E., Farmer & Stock, S. 23, T. Barry, P. O. Hickory Corners, 1857.
Willison, W., Farmer, S. 15, T. Johnstown, P. O. Lacey, 1855.
Wilson, E. D., Farmer, S. 31, T. Yankee Springs, P. O. Yankee Springs, 1871.
Wilson, A. E., Farmer, S. 33, T. Yankee Springs, P. O. Middleville, 1870.
Winans, P., Farmer, S. 36, T. Maple Grove, P. O. Nashville, 1848.
Wing, Thomas, Farmer, S. 35, T. Assyria, P. O. Bellevue, 1853.
Wing, J. F., Farmer, S. 22, T. Irving, P. O. North Irving, 1851.
Wing, Myron, Farmer, S. 26, T. Barry, P. O. Hickory Corners, 1870.
Wing, H., Farmer, S. 35, T. Barry, P. O. Hickory Corners, 1863.
Winger, John, Farmer, S. 9, T. Yankee Springs, P. O. Bowens Mills, 1866.
Winslow, J., Farmer, S. 36, T. Baltimore, P. O. Lacey, 1873.

Winslow, Geo. H., Farmer, S. 22, T. Barry, P. O. Hickory Corners, 1878.
Winslow, H. C., Dealer in Real Estate, Battle Creek.
Wolcott, Daniel, Farmer, S. 10, T. Hastings, P. O. Hastings, 1854.
Wolf, Geo., Farmer, S. 23, T. Maple Grove, P. O. Maple Grove, 1856.
Wolf, A. D., Farmer, S. 23, T. Maple Grove, P. O. Maple Grove, 1855.
Wolf, J. B., Farmer, S. 3, T. Carlton, P. O. Carlton Centre, 1852.
Wolfe, Jacob, Farmer, S. 11, T. Irving, P. O. Freeport, 1854.
Wolfe, D. W., Farmer, S. 11, T. Irving, P. O. Freeport, 1864.
Wolfe, I. J., Farmer, S. 11, T. Irving, P. O. Freeport, 1864.
Wood, J., Farmer, S. 30, T. Woodland, P. O. Coats Grove, 1846.
Wood, F., Farmer, S. 1, T. Hastings, P. O. Coats Grove, 1872.
Wood, Anson, Farmer, S. 1, T. Hastings, P. O. Coats Grove, 1844.
Wood, M., Farmer, S. 30, T. Orangeville, P. O. Prairieville, 1867.
Wood, Lewis, Farmer, S. 34, T. Assyria, P. O. Bellevue, 1852.
Woodman, T. A., Farmer, S. 11, T. Orangeville, P. O. Prairieville, 1844.
Woodmansee, G. P., Farmer, S. 34, T. Baltimore, P. O. Dowling, 1854.
Woodmansee, A. J., Farmer, S. 35, T. Baltimore, P. O. Dowling, 1861.
Woodmansee, Dr. M. C., Physician & Surgeon, Hastings, 1874.
Woodruff, J. C., Farmer, S. 14, T. Baltimore, P. O. Hastings, 1873.
Woodruff, I. C., Farmer, S. 15, T. Baltimore, P. O. Hastings, 1875.
Woodruff, C. A., Farmer, S. 1, T. Rutland, P. O. Hastings, 1874.

Wotring, J. L., Farmer, S. 11, T. Castleton, P. O. Nashville, 1866.
Wrate, John, Farmer, S. 32, T. Assyria, P. O. Bedford, 1869.
Wright, K. S., Physician & Surgeon, Freeport, 1868.
Wright, A. J., Physician, S. 22, T. Carlton, P. O. Carlton Centre, 1862.

Yarger, John, Dealer in Grain, Produce & Stock, Freeport, 1857.
Yarger, Michael, Farmer & Stock, S. 9, T. Carlton, P. O. Freeport, 1857.
Yarger, Daniel, Farmer, S. 15, T. Carlton, P. O. Carlton Centre, 1856.
Yarger, Daniel, Sr., Farmer, S. 16, T. Carlton, P. O. Carlton Centre, 1857.
Yates, Joseph C., Farmer, S. 5, T. Rutland, P. O. Irving, 1865.
Yerkley, L. A., Farmer, S. 23, T. Rutland, P. O. Hastings, 1855.
Yerkley, S., Farmer, S. 12, T. Rutland, P. O. Hastings, 1856.
Young, J. H., Farmer, S. 34, T. Hastings, P. O. Hastings, 1867.
Young, J. L., Farmer, S. 10, T. Orangeville, P. O. Prairieville, 1850.
Young, J. A., Farmer, S. 4, T. Yankee Springs, P. O. Middleville, 1849.
Yonnge, Chas., Farmer, S. 23, T. Carlton, P. O. Hastings, 1856.
Youngs, C. B., Farmer, S. 16, T. Hope, P. O. Cloverdale, 1863.
Youngs, Mary, Farmer & Stock, S. 18, T. Hope, P. O. Cloverdale, 1857.

Zerbe, Jacob, Farmer & Stock, S. 5, T. Thornapple, P. O. Caledonia, 1867.

COUNTY BUILDINGS,
Hastings. Barry County. Mich.

STATE CAPITOL,
Lansing, Mich.

Residence of MRS. H. E. LEHNNER,
Hope Township.

ST. JAMES HOTEL, Middleville, Mich.
(formerly American House)
J. N. Ollmstead, Proprietor.

J. M. ELLIOTT, M. D.,
Barry Township.

J. E. CAIRNS,
of Cairns & Brown, Dealers in General Merchandise,
Prairieville, Mich

ELI NICHOLS, Merchant,
Orangeville, Mich

WEST PINE LAKE RESORT.— JOHN T. SHELP, Proprietor
Cottages, Tents and Boats for Rent. Trading Privileges on Islands. Fine Sailing and Fishing.
Prairieville Township, Barry County, Mich.

S. M. KIDDER,
Castleton Township.

MRS. S. M. KIDDER,
Castleton Township.

JOHN YARGER,
Freeport, Mich.

WARREN FISHER,
Prairieville Township.

"THORNAPPLE LAKE RESORT,"—L. P. COLE, Proprietor.
Castleton Township, Barry County, Mich

WM. H. FORD,
Prairieville Township

MRS. SAMUEL ROUSH,
Freeport.

SAMUEL ROUSH,
Freeport.

B. W. JOHNSON, Deceased.

FARM RESIDENCE OF MYRON KILMER, Section 5, Thornapple Township.

STEPHEN TEMPLE,
Of the firm of Temple & Nelson, Gen'l Merchants,
Prairieville, Mich.

GEORGE H. NELSON.
Of the firm of Temple & Nelson, Gen'l Merchants.
Prairieville, Mich.

MR. AND MRS. FRANK PRICE,
Castleton Township.

ALBERT NUTT AND FAMILY,
Hope Township.

"MAPLE LEAF FARM."
Residence of John Wertz, Section 1, Assyria Township.

RESIDENCE OF MYRON WING,
Section 33. Barry Township.

RESIDENCE AND MILL PROPERTY OF CHARLES F. PIKE,
Section 3, Thornapple Township.

FROM L. E. HINCHMAN'S STABLES.

"OAK PARK FARM."
Residence of Mr. and Mrs. L. E. Hinchman, Section 9, Assyria Township.

ELMORE D. CLARK,
(Supervisor) Barry Township.

LEVI ROPE AND FAMILY.
Baltimore Township.

A. W. SHORTER,
Prairieville Township.

F. A. BLACKMAN,
Delton, Mich.

POLITICAL TABLE.

MR. AND MRS. BYRON WING,
Barry Township.

THE WORLD'S WEALTH, DEBT, MONEY, POPULATION, ETC.

ANALYSIS OF THE SYSTEM
—OF—
UNITED STATES LAND SURVEYS
COPYRIGHT, 1890.

METES AND BOUNDS.

U P to the time of the Revolutionary War, or until about the beginning of the present century, land, when parcelled out, and sold or granted, was described by "Metes and Bounds," and that system is still in existence in the following States, or in those portions of them which had been sold or granted when the present plan of surveys was adopted, viz., New York, Pennsylvania, New Jersey, Delaware, Maryland, Virginia, North and South Carolina, Georgia, Tennessee, Kentucky, Texas, and the six New England States. To describe land by "Metes and Bounds," is to have a known land-mark for a place of beginning, and then follow a line according to the compass-needle (or magnetic bearing), or the course of a stream, or track of an ancient highway. This plan has resulted in endless confusion and litigation, as land-marks decay and change, and it is a well-known fact that the compass-needle varies and does not always point due North.

As an example of this plan of dividing lands, the following description of a farm laid out by "Metes and Bounds," is given: "Beginning at a stone on the Bank of Doe River, at a point where the highway from A. to B. crosses said river (see point marked C. on Diagram I); thence 40° North of West 100 rods to a large stump; thence 10° North of West 80 rods; thence 15° West of North 90 rods to an oak tree (see Witness Tree on Diagram I); thence due East 120 rods to the highway; thence following the course of the highway 50 rods due North; thence 5° North of East 90 rods; thence 45° East of South 80 rods; thence 10° North of East 200 rods to the Doe River; thence following the course of the river Southwesterly to the place of beginning." This, which is a very simple and intricate description by "Metes and Bounds," would leave the boundaries of the farm as shown in Diagram I.

DIAGRAM I.

MERIDIANS AND BASE LINES.
DIAGRAM 2.

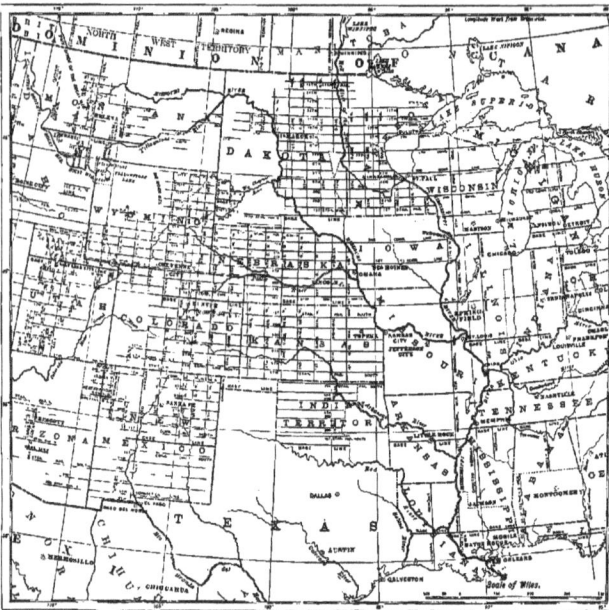

T HE present system of Governmental Land Surveys was adopted by Congress on the 7th of May, 1785. It has been the one ever since and is the legal method of describing and dividing lands. It is called the "Rectangular System," that is, all its distances and bearings are measured from two lines which are at right angles to each other, viz.:— These two lines, from which the measurements are made, are the Principal Meridians, which run North and South, and the Base Lines, which run East and West. These Principal Meridians are astronomy, by astronomical observations. Each Principal Meridian has its Base Line, and these two lines form the basis or foundation for the surveys or measurement of all the lands within the territory which they control.

Diagram 2 shows all of the Principal Meridians and Base Lines in the central portion of the United States, and from it the territory governed by each Meridian and Base Line may be readily distinguished. Each Meridian and Base Line is marked with its proper number or name, as are also the Standard Parallels and guide (or auxiliary) Meridians.

Diagram 3 illustrates what is meant when this method is termed the "Rectangular System," and how the measurements are based on lines which run at right angles to each other. The lower line running North and South (marked A. A.) represents the Principal Meridian, in this case say the 5th Principal Meridian. The lower line running East and West (marked B. B.) is the Base Line. These lines are used as the starting points or basis of all measurements or surveys made in territory controlled by the 5th Principal Meridian. The same fact applies to all other Principal Meridians and their Base Lines. Commencing at the Principal Meridian, at intervals of six miles, lines are run North and South, parallel to the Meridian. This plan is followed both East and West of the Meridian throughout the territory controlled by the Meridian.

These lines are termed "Range Lines." They divide the land into strips or divisions six miles wide, extending North and South, parallel with the Meridian. Each division is called a Range. Ranges are numbered from one upward, commencing at the Meridian; and their numbers are indicated by Roman characters. For instance, the first division (or first six miles) west of the Meridian is Range 1, West; the next is Range II., West; then comes Range III., IV., V., VI., VII., and so on, until the territory governed by another Principal Meridian is reached. In the same manner the Ranges East of the Meridian are numbered, the words East or West being always used to indicate the direction from the Principal Meridian. See Diagram 3.

Commencing at the Base Line, at intervals of six miles, lines are run East and West parallel with the Base Line. These are designated as Township Lines. They divide the land into strips or divisions six miles wide, extending East and West, parallel with the Base Line. This plan is followed both North and South of the Base Line until the territory governed by another Principal Meridian and Base Line is reached. These divisions or Townships are numbered from one upward, both North and South of the Base Line, and their numbers are indicated by figures. For instance: The first six mile division north of the Base Line is Township 1 North; the next is Township 2 North; then comes Township 3, 4, 5, and 6, North, and so on. The same plan is followed South of the Base Line; the Township being designated as Township 1 South, Township 2 South, and so on. The "North" or "South" (the initials N. or S. being generally used) indicates the direction from the Base Line. See Diagram 2.

These Township and Range Lines, crossing each other, as shown in Diagram 3, form squares, which are called "Townships" or "Government Townships," which are six miles square, or nearly that as it is possible to make them. These Townships are a very important feature in locating or describing a piece of land. The location of a Government Township, however, is very readily found when the number of the Township and Range is given, by merely counting the number indicated from the Base Line and Principal Meridian. As an example of this, Township 3 North, Range 4, West of the 4th Principal Meridian, is at once located on the square marked ✕ on Diagram 3, by counting eight tiers north of the Base Line and three west of the Meridian.

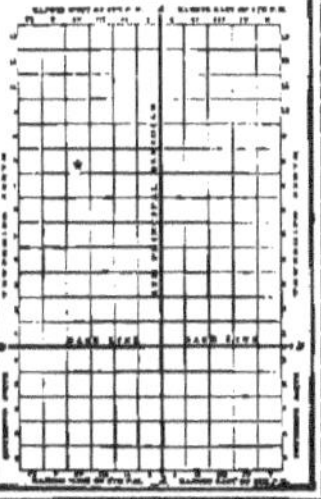

TOWNSHIPS OF LAND.

TOWNSHIPS are the largest subdivisions of land run out by the United States Surveys Township Lines are the first to be run, and a Township Corner is established every six miles and marked. This is called "Townshipping." After the Township Corners have been carefully located, the Section and Quarter Section Corners are established. Each Township is six miles square and contains 23,040 acres, or 36 square miles, as near as it is possible to make them. Thus, however, is frequently made impossible by: (1st) the presence of lakes and large streams; (2nd) by State boundaries not falling exactly on Township Lines; (3rd) by the convergence of Meridians or curvature of the earth's surface; and (4th) by inaccurate surveys.

Each Township, unless it is one of the exceptional cases referred to, is divided into 36 squares, which are called Sections. These Sections are intended to be one mile, or 320 rods, square and contain 640 acres of land. Sections are numbered consecutively from 1 to 36, as shown on Diagram 4. Beginning with Section 1 in the Northeast Corner, they run West to 6, then East to 12, then West to 18, and so on, back and forth, until they end with Section 36 in the Southeast Corner.

Diagram 4 shows a plat of a Township as it is divided and platted by the government surveyors. These Townships are called Government Township or Congressional Townships, to distinguish them from Civil Townships or organized Townships, as frequently the lines of organized Townships do not conform to the Government Township lines.

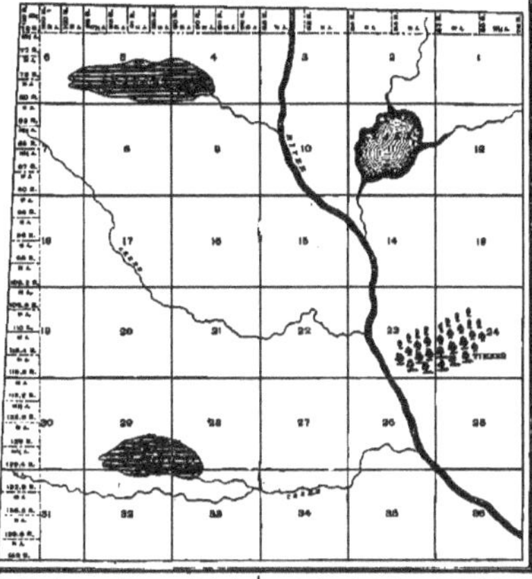

SECTIONS OF LAND.

DIAGRAM 5 illustrates how a section may be subdivided, although the Diagram only gives a few of the many subdivisions into which a section may be divided. All Sections (except fractional Sections) are supposed to be 320 rods, or one mile, square and therefore contain 640 acres—a number easily divisible. Sections are subdivided into fractional parts to suit the convenience of the owners of the land. A half-section contains 320 acres, a quarter-section contains 160 acres; half of a quarter contains 80 acres, and quarter of a quarter-section contains 40 acres, and so on. Each piece of land is described according to the portion of the section which it embraces—as the Northeast quarter of the 10, or the Southeast quarter of the Southeast quarter of Section 10. Diagram 5 shows how many of these subdivisions are platted, and also shows the plan of designating and describing them by initial letters at each parcel of land on the Diagram is marked with its description.

As has already been stated, all Sections (except Fractional Sections which are explained elsewhere) are supposed to contain 640 acres, and even though mistakes have been made in surveying, as it frequently the case, making sections larger or smaller than 640 acres, the Government recognizes no variation, but sells or grants each regular section as containing 640 acres "more or less."

The Government Surveyors are not required to subdivide sections by running lines within them, but they usually establish Quarter Posts on Section Lines on each side of a section at the points marked A, B, C, and D, on Diagram 5. After establishing Township corners, Section Lines are the next to be run, and section corners are established. When these are carefully located the Quarter Posts are located at points nearly equidistant between Section Corners as possible. These corners when established let the Government Surveyors cannot be changed, even though it is positively shown that mistakes have been made which cause some sections or quarter sections to be either larger or smaller than others. The laws, however, of all the States provide certain rules for local surveyors to follow in dividing Sections into smaller parcels of land than has been outlined in the Government corners. For instance, in dividing a quarter section into two parcels, the distance between the Government Corners is carefully measured and the new post is located at a point equidistant between them. This plan is followed in running out "eighties," "fortieths," "twenties," etc. In this way, if the Government division overruns or falls short, each portion gains or loses its proportion. This is not the case, however, with Fractional Sections along the North or West sides of a Township, or adjoining a lake or large stream.

DIAGRAM 5.

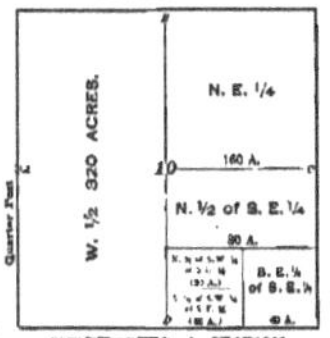

SUBDIVIDING A SECTION.

DIAGRAM 4

FRACTIONAL PIECES OF LAND.

CONGRESSIONAL Townships vary continually as to size and boundaries. Mistakes made in surveying and the fact that Meridians converge as they run North cause every Township to vary more or less from the 23,040 acres which a perfect Township would contain. See Diagram 4. In arranging a Township into Sections all the surplus or deficiency of land is given to, or taken from, the North and West tiers of Sections. In other words, all Sections in the Township are made full—640 acres—except those on the North and West, which are given all the land that is left after forming the other 23 Sections.

Diagram 4 illustrates how the surplus or deficiency of land inside of these Sections is distributed and the Sections it affects. It will be seen that Sections 1, 2, 3, 4, 5, 6, 7, 18, 19, 30 and 31, are the "Fractional Sections," or the Sections which are affected if the Township overruns or falls short. Inside of these Fractional Sections, all of the surplus or deficiency of land (over or under 640 acres) is carried to the "forties" or "eighties" that touch the Township Line. These pieces of land are called "Fractional Forties" or "Fractional Eighties," as the case may be. Diagrams 4 and 6 show the manner of marking the acreage and enclosing the boundaries of these "Fractions."

Diagram 6 illustrates how the surplus or deficiency of land inside of these Sections is distributed and which "forties" or "eighties" it affects. From this arrangement it will be seen that in any Section that touches the North or West Township Line, the southeast Quarter may be full—160 acres—while another quarter of the same Section may be much larger or smaller. Frequently these fractional "forties" or "eighties" are listed as shown in Diagram 6. They are always described as fractional tracts of land, as the fractional N. W. ¼ of Section 6, "etc. Of course these portions of these Sections which are not affected by these variations are described in the usual manner—as Southeast ¼ of Section 6. As a rule Townships are narrower at the North than at the South side. The Meridians of Longitude (which run North and South) converge as they run North and South from the Equator. They begin at the Equator with bases even then and gradually converge until they all meet at the poles. Now, as the Range lines run both North and South, it will at once be seen that the convergence of Meridians will cause every Congressional Township (North of the Equator) to be narrower at its North than at its South side, as stated. See Diagram 4. In addition to this fact, mistakes of measurement are constantly and almost unavoidably made in running both Township and Range lines, and if no new starting points were established the lines would become confused and unreliable, and the size and shape of Townships materially affected by the time the surveys had extended over a hundred miles from the Base Line and Principal Meridian. In order to correct the surveys and variations caused by the allowance of latitude and to straighten the lines, "Correction Lines" (or Guide Meridians and Standard Parallels) are established at frequent intervals, usually as follows: North of the Base Line a Correction Line is run East and West parallel with the Base Line, usually every twenty-four miles. South of the Base Line a Correction Line is usually established every thirty miles. Both East and West of the Principal Meridian "Correction Lines" are usually established every 48 miles. All Correction Lines are located by careful measurement, and the succeeding surveys are based upon them.

DIAGRAM 6.

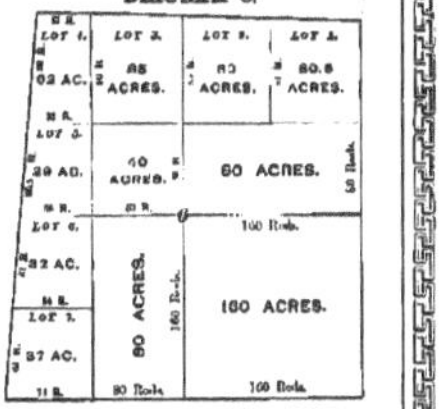

PLAT OF A FRACTIONAL SECTION.

DIAGRAM 3.

DIGEST OF THE SYSTEM
OF
CIVIL GOVERNMENT,

WITH A REVIEW OF THE

DUTIES AND POWERS OF THE PRINCIPAL OFFICIALS CONNECTED
WITH THE VARIOUS BRANCHES OF NATIONAL, STATE,
COUNTY AND TOWNSHIP GOVERNMENT.

NATIONAL GOVERNMENT.

He also has oversight over several of the Government's charitable and benevolent institutions. For the purpose of handling properly the business connected with most of the subjects mentioned, there are bureaus organized for the purpose.

The salaries paid to the principal officials connected with the Interior Department are as follows: This assistant secretary of the Interior, $4,000 per year; assistant secretary, $4,000; chief clerk, $2,750; assistant attorney-general, $5,000; commissioner of the General Land Office, $4,000; commissioner of Indian affairs, $4,000; superintendent of Indian schools, $3,000; commissioner of the Pension Office, $5,000; medical referee, $3,000; commissioner of railroads, $4,500; commissioner of the Patent Office, $5,000; commissioner of the Education Office, $3,000; director of geological survey, $6,000; superintendent of the Census Office, $6,000.

DEPARTMENT OF AGRICULTURE.

This department was formerly connected with the Interior Department, but in 1889 it was reorganized and made independent, and the Secretary of Agriculture was made a member of the Cabinet. The head of this department is appointed by the President, and receives a salary of $8,000 per annum.

The general duty and design of the Department of Agriculture is to acquire and diffuse among the people of the United States useful information on subjects connected with agriculture in the most general and comprehensive sense of that word, and to procure, propagate and distribute among the people new and valuable seeds and plants.

The following is a list of the chief officials connected with the Department of Agriculture and their salaries, and the list will also serve to indicate the various lines of work handled by and the various duties which devolve upon the department, viz.: Assistant secretary of agriculture receives $4,000 per annum; chief of Weather Bureau, $4,000; chief of Bureau of Animal Industry, $2,500; statistician, $2,500; chemist, $2,500; botanist, $2,500; ornithologist, $2,500; chief of forestry division, $2,000; pomologist, $2,500; chief of vegetable pathology division, $2,500; entomologist, $2,500; director of office of experiment stations, $3,000; chief division of accounts, $2,000; chief of division of records and editing, $2,000; chief of division of illustrations and engravings, $2,000; horticulturist, $2,500.

DEPARTMENT OF JUSTICE.

The head of the Department of Justice is the Attorney-General who is appointed by the President, and receives a salary of $8,000 per annum. The principal assistant of the Attorney-General is the Solicitor-General, who receives $7,000 per year. There are a number of assistant attorneys-general who receive $5,000 per annum, and a special assistant attorney-general is appointed for nearly all of the various departments, including the Treasury, State, Post Office and Interior Departments. Besides these there are a number of special officials connected with the Department of Justice, such as examiner of titles, who receives $3,750 per annum; superintendent of buildings, $2,100; appointment and disbursing clerk, $2,000, and attorney in charge of pardons, $2,000.

The Attorney-General is the legal adviser of the President, and it is the duty of the Department of Justice to give all opinions and render all services requiring the skill of persons learned in the law necessary to enable the President and other officers of the various Government departments to discharge their respective duties. This department is also required to prosecute or defend all suits or proceedings in which the United States is interested. The Attorney-General has general supervision over all the solicitors for the various departments; but the several district attorneys throughout the United States are under the direct control of this department; and United States district attorneys of all the districts of the United States and Territories.

INDEPENDENT DEPARTMENTS.

There are several independent departments, which, although some of them are as important as the foregoing, and their heads are not Cabinet members, yet they form a very necessary part and extend to very important branches of the National Government.

Government Printing Office. The head of the branch of public work is the Public Printer, who is appointed by the President, and receives a salary of $4,500 per year. His chief clerk is paid $2,400 per year, and there is a foreman of printing and a foreman of binding, each of whom receive $2,100 per annum.

Civil Service Commission. This commission consists of three commissioners, each of whom are paid $3,500 per year. The chief examiner connected with the commission is paid $3,000 per annum, and the secretary $2,000.

Interstate Commerce Commission. This commission was created for the purpose, and charged with the duty, of seeing that the laws regulating interstate commerce were faithfully executed and observed, and to prevent unjust discrimination on the part of railway corporations and common carriers. The commission consists of five commissioners appointed from different sections of the United States, each of whom receives a salary of $7,500 per year. The secretary of the commission receives a salary of $3,500 per annum.

Department of Labor. The general design of this department is to collect, assort and systematize statistical details relating to the different branches of labor in the United States. The head of this department is known as the Commissioner of the Department of Labor, and he is paid a salary of $5,000 per annum. His chief clerk receives $2,000 per year, and disbursing clerk $1,800.

JUDICIARY.

The judicial powers of the United States are vested in the following named courts, viz: The United States Supreme Court, consisting of one chief justice and eight associate justices; the United States Court of Claims, which consists of one chief justice and four judges; the United States Circuit Court of Appeals; and the United States District and District Courts. All judges of United States Courts are appointed for life, or during "good behavior." The chief justice of the United States Supreme Court receives a salary of $10,500 per annum, and the associate justices $10,000 each. The circuit judges receive a salary of $6,000 each per annum, district judges $5,000, and judges of the Court of Claims $4,500 each per year.

The jurisdiction of the United States Courts extends to all cases in law and in equity arising under the Constitution, the laws of the United States, and treaties; to all cases affecting ambassadors, other public ministers and consuls; to all cases of admiralty and maritime jurisdiction; to controversies to which the United States shall be a party; to controversies between two or more States; between a State and citizens of another State; between citizens of different States; between citizens of the same State claiming lands under grants of different States; between a State, or the citizens thereof, and foreign States, citizens or subjects. In all cases affecting ambassadors, other public ministers and consuls, and those to which a State is a party, the Supreme Court has original jurisdiction. In the other cases the Supreme Court has appellate jurisdiction.

LEGISLATIVE DEPARTMENT.

The legislative powers of the United States are vested in a Congress, which consists of a Senate and House of Representatives, and which meets annually in Washington on the first Monday in December. The constitution given to Congress the following general powers: To lay and collect taxes, duties, imposts and excises; pay the debts of the United States; borrow money on the credit of the United States; regulate commerce; to establish uniform laws on naturalization and bankruptcy; to coin money and regulate the value thereof; fix the stand-

ard of weights and measures; to declare war; to raise and support armies that it is provided that no appropriation for that purpose can be for a longer period than the two years); to provide and maintain a navy; to grant letters of marque and reprisal, and make rules concerning captures on land and water; to make rules for the government and regulation of the land and naval forces; to establish postoffices and post-roads; to promote the progress of science and the useful arts by securing for limited times, to authors and inventors, the exclusive right to their respective writings and discoveries; to constitute tribunals inferior to the Supreme Court; to define and punish piracies and felonies committed on the high seas and offenses against the law of nations; to exercise exclusive legislation over the District of Columbia and places purchased for forts, magazines, arsenals, etc.; and further to make all laws necessary for the general welfare of the United States, and for "carrying into execution the foregoing powers, and all other powers vested by the Constitution in the Government of the United States, or in any department or officer thereof." The Constitution expressly forbids Congress making any law respecting the establishment of religion, or prohibiting the free exercise thereof, or abridging the freedom of speech, or of the press, or the right of the people peaceably to assemble, and to petition the Government for a redress of grievances. Congress cannot suspend the privilege of the writ of habeas corpus (except in cases of rebellion or invasion when the public safety may require it. No bill of attainder or ex post facto law can be passed. No tax or duty can be laid on articles exported from any State. No preference can be given by any regulation of commerce or revenue to the ports of one State over those of another. No title of nobility can be granted. Every law passed by Congress must be submitted to the President for his approval. If he returns it with his objections, or vetoes it, the measure may be passed over his veto by a two-thirds vote of both branches of Congress. The Senate, or the "Upper House of Congress," is composed of two Senators from each State in the Union, who are elected by the Legislatures of their respective States, for the term of six years, and receive a salary of $5,000 per annum. No person can be elected to the United States Senate who has not attained the age of thirty years, been nine years a citizen of the United States, and is not when elected an inhabitant of the State from which he is chosen. The Senate has exclusive power in all impeachments, its consent and confirmation is necessary for all important officers appointed by the President. Its consent is also necessary to conclude any treaty.

The House of Representatives is the "Lower House of Congress." Each State in the Union is divided into congressional districts of as nearly equal population as is practicable. In each district a representative is elected by the people for a term of two years, and each is paid a salary of $5,000 per year. Besides these, a delegate from each Territory is admitted to the House of Representatives, who is not qualified to vote, but has the right to debate on all subjects in which the Territory which he represents has an interest. No person can be a representative who has not attained the age of twenty-five years, been for seven years a citizen of the United States, and is at the time of his election an inhabitant of the State from which he is chosen. All bills for raising revenue must originate in the House of Representatives.

STATE GOVERNMENT.

THE method of State government throughout the United States follows very closely the general plan of government that prevails in national affairs. The various functions of government in State affairs are handled in dependencies, each a State affair, as in the head of each branch, and the lines of work are divided between the executive, legislative and judicial powers. All the States are governed under a constitution, which outlines and defines the powers which each of these departments shall exercise and possess. All of the most important State officials are elected by the people, for terms of the State government. The chief executive officer in all of the States of the Union, and is elected for a direct term of the people. The term of office varies materially in the different States, ranging from two to six years. As in the matter of salary that the Governor receives, it also differs widely throughout the different States and is subject to frequent change. At the present writing two States—New York and Pennsylvania—pay their Governors $10,000 per year; Illinois and California both pay $6,000 per annum; Minnesota, Indiana, Kentucky, Massachusetts, Missouri, Nevada, New Jersey, Virginia and Wisconsin all pay $5,000 per year; Maryland pays $4,500; Michigan, Louisiana, Pennsylvania, Texas and Tennessee $4,000 each; Florida and California both pay $3,500 per annum; Minnesota, Indiana, North Carolina all pay $3,000; West Virginia, $2,700; Montana and Washington, $5,000; the Dakotas and Nebraska, $2,500; Connecticut, Delaware and Maine, $2,000; Oregon, $1,500, and New Hampshire, Vermont and Rhode Island $1,000 each. About the only statutory concerning the qualifications required for this office that is common to all the States is that he must be a citizen of the State in which he is elected. In most of the States, in addition to his salary named, the Governor is furnished with a residence, which is known as the "Executive Mansion."

The powers and duties that devolve upon the Governor are about the same in all of the States. He is charged with a general supervision over the faithful execution of the laws, and is the legal guardian of all the property of the State not specifically entrusted in other officers by law, and is authorized to take summary proceedings in all such matters. He is expected to communicate by message to each session of the State legislature such information or recommendation regarding State affairs as he may deem necessary and proper, and he is empowered in all cases sessions of that body whenever the public welfare may demand. He is empowered by the laws of nearly all the States to grant reprieves, commutations and pardons to all persons convicted of offenses against the State, treason and impeachment excepted. He also has the power to fill by appointment all vacancies in any office which may occur by reason of death, resignation or otherwise. He may require the opinion of the respective officers of the State government in writing, upon any subject relating to their respective offices, and examines and approves the bonds of State officials. In many States the Governor has power to grant reprieves and pardons, after conviction, for all offenses against the State except in cases of impeachment; but a few States the pardoning power is vested in a board selected for that purpose, of which the Governor is generally a member. The Governor has the appointment of a number of State officers, and in many cases if an elective office becomes vacant he has the power to fill it by appointment, his power to appoint a State officer, or even an officer, is subject to restriction by the Legislature or General Assembly, and in other cases requires the confirmation of other bodies before persons charged with filling vacancies in other State offices, and he has power to veto warrants for fleeing criminals upon requisition of other Governors.

LIEUTENANT-GOVERNOR.

The office of Lieutenant-Governor does not exist in all of the States in the Union, as less than under that name in about one-half of the States. The office is only known as the President of the State Senate. In most of the States the Lieutenant-Governor is paid a certain amount per day during sessions of the Legislature or General Assembly, and in others he is allowed a fixed salary; but it is provided that if the duties of Gov-

ernor should devolve upon him, he shall during the continuance of such emergency be entitled to the emoluments thereof. The principal duty of the Lieutenant-Governor is to act as the presiding officer of the State Senate or Upper House of the State Legislature. In case a vacancy should occur in the office of Governor, the Lieutenant-Governor would act as Governor until such vacancy was filled by election; and in all cases where the Lieutenant-Governor is unable to act as presiding officer of the Senate, a President pro tempore is chosen by that body. The Lieutenant-Governor has no vote in the Senate except in cases of a tie or equal division of the members.

SECRETARY OF STATE.

The office of Secretary of State is one of the most important offices within the gift of the people of a State, and the office name under that name in every State in the Union. The Secretary of State may be said to be the official secretary of the Governor, and of all the documents issued by the chief executive, and he is the custodian of the Great Seal of the State. As a rule it is the duty of the Secretary of State to call the House of Representatives to order and preside until a temporary presiding officer, or Speaker, is elected. It is also his duty that bills are prepared for the Legislature or General Assembly; he compares the legislative manual and tables it to be printed and distributed; governs the printing and distribution of the State laws; indexes and files complete documents; provides and distributes election blanks; has charge of all bonds, bills, papers, etc., of the Legislature, and is practically "keeper of all public acts, laws, records, bonds, etc." The Secretary of State is required to keep a register of all the official acts of the Governor, and affixes the Seal of the State to all official documents; etc., keeps a record of them, and is obliged to give any person a copy of the same when requested. It is the duty that the Secretary of State is ex-officio member of a number of the official State boards, but no list of these could be given that would apply to all States, as they are different in the various States.

STATE AUDITOR.

The office of Auditor of State exists under one name or another in nearly every State in the Union. The title of this officer, however, is not alike in all the States, as in many of them, notably California, Connecticut, Florida, Georgia, Maryland, Nevada, New Jersey, New York, South Carolina, Tennessee, Texas and a few others, it is known as State Comptroller. In a few of the States, including Michigan and Pennsylvania, the office is called Auditor-General, and in two of the States the public accounts are audited by a Board of Auditors. In all the States, however, the duties that devolve upon this branch of the State government are practically the same, and a general explanation of the scope of work handled by the State Auditor in one State will apply, except as regards minor details, to all of the States. It is the duty of the State Auditor to keep the accounts of the State with any other State or Territory, and with the United States and all public officers, corporations and individuals having accounts with his State. He audits the accounts of all public officers who are to be paid out of the State Treasury, and all persons who are authorized to receive money out of the State Treasury. In fact, all claims against the State, which are to be paid out of the State Treasury must be presented to the Auditor, who, after the same is adjusted, issues warrants therefor payable at the Treasury. A complete record of such warrant is kept by the Auditor, who also keeps an account with the State Treasurer, charging him with all moneys paid into the Treasury and giving credit for all warrants paid, and the books and vouchers of the Treasury must balance therewith. An account is also made between these two officers at stated intervals. In a number of the States the Auditor is charged with a greater number of duties, such as auditing the revenues of the State, the assessment and collection of all taxes of different kinds, and the keeping of the railroad records; in which case he has an assistant who is known as the Deputy Auditor, or State Auditor.

STATE TREASURER.

This is one of the most important executive offices in the gift of the people of a State. The State Treasurer handles vast sums of the people's money, and as a rule is very heavily bonded, ranging from $500,000 up into the millions, as required of him and generally the Governor is empowered to demand additional bonds or security from him whenever the condition of the funds insufficiently to fully protect the State.

The duties of the State Treasurer are implied by the title of the office, and they are very much the same throughout all of the States of the Union. The State Treasurer is custodian of all the State funds. He deposits and has charge of all the funds belonging to the State; he deposits these funds in banks, which gives bonds to secure the Treasurer, or taxes against tax, and which pay interest on such balances. The State Treasurer pays out State funds only on warrants issued or approved by the State Auditor, or the equivalent of his office. In some States, therefore, the warrants passing of the Auditor and his or some similar officer first before payment can be legally made. The State Treasurer makes reports to the Governor and the Legislature in relation to the condition of the funds and all matters of his office. He keeps a record of all moneys received and paid out of the various "funds," which "funds" must be kept separate in accounts. In nearly all of the States the State Treasurer is ex-officio member of a number of official boards, and to some degree corresponds to the provisions in relation to the conduct of national financial matters in some of the States, as the United States Treasurer and one or two other State officials constitute a board, which acts as a trustee, managing and control over the investment and sinking funds and makes all the investments of State moneys. Besides this office, a double system is carried on—both Auditor and Treasurer keeping a full record of all moneys received and paid out, and their books and accounts must balance, as a general rule, where they must be checked, as against another, yet in some States the Auditor and Treasurer are separately so independent of each other that the checking of one against the other takes practically a matter of course, which must be frequently done given credit for allowances. In still other States the Treasurer keeps a full account of the various "funds," which "funds" must be kept separate in accounts. In nearly all of the States the State Treasurer and ascertains the amount of funds in the Treasury.

ATTORNEY-GENERAL.

The Attorney-General is, as the name implies, the general legal counsel or lawyer for the State government. He is charged with a general supervision of all of the State's law business, and in all of the States she powers and duties of the Attorney-General are very much similar. It is his duty to appear for the State in all cases and proceedings in the Supreme Court in which the State has an interest; to prosecute or defend such suits, either for or against a State officer in which the State is interested, or in the name of the State; and to give legal advice and opinions upon all matters relating to the various official duties, and when public interest requires him to render his official opinion in cases relating to the administration of the various State institutions and the conduct of official business. It is his duty to see that the various county or state's attorneys throughout the State in the discharge of their duties; and it is required to assist them or prosecute such legal matters when the public interest so requires. Attorneys and county attorneys. It is also his duty to represent the State in the various suits and prosecution of suits or proceedings relating to the subjects in which the State is interested. He is required to render his opinions upon the questions of funds appropriated in the various State institutions, and prosecute breaches of trust in the administration of the state; and when-

STATE SUPERINTENDENT OR SUPERINTENDENT OF PUBLIC INSTRUCTION.

STATE LIBRARIAN.

ADJUTANT-GENERAL.

PUBLIC EXAMINERS OR BANK EXAMINERS.

COMMISSIONER OR SUPERINTENDENT OF INSURANCE.

COMMISSIONERS OF LABOR STATISTICS.

OTHER STATE OFFICERS.

STATE BOARDS.

LEGISLATURE OR GENERAL ASSEMBLY.

SENATE.

HOUSE OF REPRESENTATIVES.

JUDICIARY.

COUNTY GOVERNMENT.

AUDITING OFFICER AND CLERK OF THE COUNTY BOARD.

COUNTY TREASURER.

COUNTY RECORDER OR REGISTER OF DEEDS.

DIGEST OF THE SYSTEM OF CIVIL GOVERNMENT.

CIRCUIT OR DISTRICT CLERK, OR CLERK OF COURT.

SHERIFF.

COUNTY SUPERINTENDENT OR COMMISSIONER OF SCHOOLS.

COUNTY, PROSECUTING OR STATE'S ATTORNEY.

PROBATE OR COUNTY JUDGE.

COUNTY SURVEYOR.

COUNTY CORONER.

OTHER COUNTY OFFICERS.

COUNTY BOARD.

TOWNSHIP GOVERNMENT.

SCHOOL DISTRICT GOVERNMENT.

CITIES AND VILLAGES.

GENERAL INFORMATION
on
Banking and Business Methods.

RELATIONS BETWEEN A BANK AND ITS CUSTOMERS.

OPENING AN ACCOUNT.

DEPOSITS.

DISCOUNTS, LOANS, ETC.

COLLECTIONS.

STATEMENTS AND BALANCES.

NEGOTIABLE PAPER.

PROMISSORY NOTES.

BILLS OF EXCHANGE.

CHECKS.

DRAFTS.

ENDORSEMENT.

GENERAL INFORMATION ON BANKING AND BUSINESS METHODS.

GUARANTY.

ACCOMMODATION PAPER.

IDENTIFICATION.

RECEIPTS AND RELEASES.

DRAFTS AND DRAWEES.

AGENCY.

FORMS AND METHOD OF PARTIES.

CLEARING HOUSE.

www.ingramcontent.com/pod-product-compliance
Lightning Source LLC
Chambersburg PA
CBHW021417090426

42742CB00009B/1169